# Death and Probate

# Death and Probate

*A self-help guide to managing
the procedures yourself*

**GORDON BOWLEY**

**howto**books

Published by How To Books Ltd,
3 Newtec Place, Magdalen Road,
Oxford OX4 1RE. United Kingdom.
Tel: (01865) 793806. Fax: (01865) 248780.
email: info@howtobooks.co.uk
www.howtobooks.co.uk

British Library Cataloguing in Publication Data
A catalogue record for this book is available from
the British Library

Produced for How To Books by Deer Park Productions
Typeset by TW Typesetting, Plymouth, Devon
Printed and bound by Cromwell Press, Trowbridge, Wiltshire

NOTE: The material contained in this book is set out in good
faith for general guidance and no liability can be accepted for
loss or expense incurred as a result of relying in particular
circumstances on statements made in the book. Laws and
regulations are complex and liable to change, and readers
should check the current position with the relevant
authorities before making personal arrangements.

# Contents

# Preface

For over thirty years I practised as a family solicitor and was much engaged in the fields of probate and wills. It became obvious to me that the majority of the cases I handled in these fields could have been dealt with by any reasonably intelligent layperson who had time available and a little professional guidance. In fact, in many solicitors' offices, executives and their assistants do much of the work involved in dealing with the estates of those who die. Of course there are other cases which require a great deal of legal knowledge and training, but these are the exceptional ones.

Some years after retirement, I had occasion as executor of a friend's will to wind up a large estate and because of the sheer volume of work it involved, I decided to employ a firm of solicitors (not my old firm). When I was told the basis on which their fees would be calculated I discovered that times had changed. I was so appalled by the fees that there and then I decided to write out for my family a step-by-step guide to the procedures to follow and the information that would be required to wind up my affairs when I die, without the necessity for professional help.

Those writings became this work and I hope that both they and you will find it of use and a great money-saver!

This book is not intended to deal with every eventuality, but I believe it will cover what needs to be known in the majority of 'ordinary' cases. It does not deal with the calculation of inheritance tax, but if you decide to deal with the estate yourself rather than employ a solicitor, the Personal Applications Section of the Probate Registry will arrange for the tax to be worked out for you. No attempt has been made to cover estates involving life interests in great detail or foreign property, but throughout I have indicated where I consider professional assistance should be invoked. When deciding whether to deal with an estate yourself rather than hand it over to a solicitor, bear in mind that if you get stuck, you can always seek legal advice on a specific point or instruct a solicitor to handle a particular stage – for example, you might wish to write all the letters and only ask the solicitor to prepare and lodge the probate forms. Such a course would reduce the cost considerably and I have included suitable specimen letters with relevant addresses in the appendices.

In spite of its limitations, I honestly think that this book includes all that it is necessary to know to enable the intelligent novice, with the necessary time available, to wind up most estates in England or Wales.

Go to it and good luck!

*Author's notes*
- This book only deals with the law applicable to England and Wales. Scottish law is different. Moreover, law and practice do change frequently and while every effort has been made to ensure that the contents of this short work are accurate and up to date, no responsibility is accepted for any loss resulting from

acting, or from failure to act, as a result of it and the book is bought and sold on that basis.

◆ Throughout the book, 'he' should be read as 'she' or 'they' where the context and circumstances require.

◆ The Department for Work and Pensions and the administration of Social Security Benefits were reorganised in April 2002.

Benefits for people of pensionable age will be dealt with in the future by the new Pensions Service and benefits for those of working age will be dealt with by the Employment Service operating from the Job Centre.

Claims for benefit from the Social Fund will be dealt with by the Employment Service offices irrespective of the age of the claimant.

Because these changes are being rolled out gradually over different parts of the country it is not possible to generalise and state which arrangements will be in force in any particular part of the country at any particular time. Accordingly when reading this book it might be necessary to construe references to the Benefits Agency as references to the Pensions Service or to the Employment Service.

# Part 1

# How to Proceed
# on a Death

# 1

# Dying

## DEATH

Most people die naturally as the result of organ failure or disease; others suffer accidental deaths and yet others die as the result of the action or inaction of themselves or of others. Modern developments in medicine have given us the opportunity to control the time and manner of our dying to an extent which would have been unimaginable to our grandparents and these developments have also inevitably thrown up hitherto undreamt of legal, sociological and philosophical problems. Indeed, modern medical developments have blurred the distinction between life and death. For our grandparents death occurred when the heart ceased to beat and the lungs to breathe, but today heartbeat, breathing and body nourishment can be artificially sustained even after the brain has died. Is a person in such a condition alive or dead?

There is little of extraordinary note to be said about the legal aspects of dying naturally after one's allotted span. When interference with the course of nature occurs the legal consequences for all concerned differ considerably according to the circumstances of each case and what form of interference takes place. This book is not intended to cover sociological or philosophical matters. It is intended to be a brief practical guide to point the layman along the road to what he can, cannot and should do and indicate how he might do it.

## CAN ONE CHOOSE THE TIME OR MANNER OF ONE'S DEATH?

Until the passing of the 1961 Suicide Act suicide and attempted suicide were criminal offences in the United Kingdom, although there was not much that could be done about it if it was successful. Today suicide is no longer a criminal offence, but life insurance policies will not pay out in such cases.

Although suicide is not a criminal offence, assisting suicide is. The Director of Public Prosecutions may seek the imprisonment for up to 14 years of anyone who aids, abets, counsels or procures the suicide of another or an attempt by another to commit suicide. No matter how heart-rending the circumstances, euthanasia (sometimes called mercy killing) is also illegal and because of the rule that no one can profit financially from their own crime, anyone who engages in mercy killing not only risks imprisonment but will be unable to inherit from the deceased's estate.

The positive act of killing without the deceased's consent is, of course, always illegal under English law, but there is generally no obligation to act to attempt to save a life unless one has expressly or impliedly undertaken such an obligation, as in the case of, for example, a doctor in relation to his patient. If the obligation has been under-taken it cannot legally be shed without the proper consent of the person in respect of whom it has been undertaken, unless one makes arrangements for another to undertake it. For a doctor to withdraw treatment with the patient's consent is not a criminal or a civil offence.

In cases of terminal illness there is sometimes a narrow distinction between assisting suicide and the withdrawal of medical treatment; the one involves the introduction of an external element which causes death and the other allows causes which are already present in the body to cause death. In cases of doubt the guidance of a court can be sought in advance.

It is a principle of English law that, as one judge has put it, 'a mentally competent patient has an absolute right to consent or refuse consent to medical treatment for any reason, rational or irrational, or for no reason at all even where that decision may lead to his or her own death.' The question is one of the right to self-determination and not what is in the patient's best interest. For others, such as doctors, to override the patient's wishes is 'benevolent paternalism' and an assault. For this reason, although there is no relevant Act of Parliament, the common law recognises living wills or advance directives as they are sometimes called.

## LIVING WILLS

A living will is a document which is made by a mentally competent person and which sets out what medical treatment that person wishes, or does not wish, to undergo in specified circumstances. Living wills are useful in that they may be relied upon if at a future date the maker loses the powers of making decisions or communication, e.g. as a result of falling into a coma or suffering a stroke. They can assist relatives and doctors to achieve the correct decision and save them from much worry about what the patient would wish when agonising decisions have to be made.

To be valid a living will must be freely made by a person at least 18 years old at the time the will is made. It must be voluntarily made, without pressure, influence or encouragement by another. The person making the will must not be rendered mentally incapable of reaching a balanced judgement when the will is made by reason of illness, mental distress or anything else. The living will should clearly state the nature of the treatment and circumstances in which it is to be acted upon and that the nature of the treatment, the circumstances in which it is to be acted upon and the likely effect of the treatment are fully understood by the person making it. The will must not have been revoked, even orally, by the time the question of carrying out the treatment arises and if tested in a court, the court will take into account, but not necessarily follow, the patient's orally expressed wishes, even if the patient is under the age of 18.

If a living will is made it should be frequently reviewed because one's wishes may change in the light of advances in medical science and care should be taken to ensure that the will and any changes to it are known to the medical practitioner, e.g. by lodging it with him. Discussing the will with the family members could lead to suggestions of undue influence having been applied by them.

A specimen form of living will is included in Appendix 1.

## CAPACITY TO DECIDE

Interesting legal questions arise when one does not make an uninfluenced, informed decision to shorten or lengthen the natural length of one's life or is adjudged not to have sufficient mental capacity to make such a decision. Similar problems arise when, having such capacity and having made the decision, one lacks the physical ability to carry the decision out.

As stated above, a doctor who has in his care a terminally ill but mentally competent patient whom the doctor treats without the patient's consent commits a civil and a criminal assault upon the patient, but what constitutes treatment and what is the position if the patient is not in a position to make a proper decision and has not previously given a proper advance directive on the subject which remains unchanged?

Treatment must be distinguished from a withdrawal of basic care such as washing and feeding by spoon as opposed to artificial feeding. Withdrawal of basic care is not permitted; withdrawal of treatment is sometimes permitted.

## ACTION IN THE PATIENT'S BEST INTEREST

In a case in which there is no proper consent or refusal and the patient is incapable of giving any, the doctor must do what is in the best interest of the patient. In the case of an adult patient it is for the doctor to make an informed decision in the light of general medical opinion as to what the patient's best interest is, although in cases of any doubt he should seek advice from a court. If the patient is a child or a ward of court it is for the court to decide, but the child's views and the parents' views will usually be taken into consideration. In neither case is it for a carer or member of the family to decide what is in the patient's best interest.

For a doctor to switch off a life-support machine or withhold artificial feeding or other treatment from an insensate terminally ill patient who has left no valid instructions is not a criminal or civil offence if the doctor considers it is in the patient's best interest. This is because in withdrawing the treatment the doctor is fulfilling his duty to act in the patient's best interest and not introducing an external element but rather ceasing to treat (omission not commission) and allowing the patient to die of the pre-existing condition. It is not the withdrawal of the support system but the pre-existing condition which kills. A doctor who uses drugs to reduce a terminally ill patient's suffering in the belief that to do so is in the patient's best interest and incidentally hastens the moment of death may be justified in doing so, but administering a drug with the primary purpose of ending a patient's life is unlawful whether or not it is the patient's wish and whether or not the doctor considers it to be in the patient's best interest.

## IS THERE A RIGHT TO DIE?

Withdrawal of or failure to supply medical treatment with the patient's proper consent or at the patient's request is not to be confused with the patient having a right to die, even if death will inevitably follow. The European Court has recently confirmed in the case of *Pretty* v *The United Kingdom* that there is no general right to die as such in English law. If the patient is mentally competent but physically incapable, a general right to die would involve the assistance of others in the withdrawal of basic care or the introduction of a positive element with the primary intention of causing death, both of which are unlawful euthanasia.

## INTENTIONALLY AND ACCIDENTALLY CAUSING DEATH

For a doctor to withdraw or fail to supply medical treatment with the patient's proper consent or at the patient's request is not the same thing as for a third party to surreptitiously disconnect a life-support system: the doctor is allowing the patient to die from the pre-existing condition but the third party is preventing the doctor from prolonging the patient's life.

To cause another's death intentionally and without lawful justification constitutes murder, or if the death is caused without intention but with gross negligence, manslaughter, and in either case there is a civil assault giving a right to damages which survives the death.

If the death of another is caused unintentionally and without negligence it is accidental death for which there is no civil or criminal liability, unless the act which caused the death was in breach of a duty imposed upon the perpetrator by statute, in which case there are both criminal and civil liabilities. To cause the death of another by an act which is not gross negligence but which could be foreseen to cause harm but not necessarily death, is a civil offence which gives rise to a claim for damages.

## FAILURE TO ASSIST

A failure to assist another which results in death does not incur a liability for damages or criminal liability, unless the person who fails to act has undertaken a duty of care to the person who dies, e.g. as in the doctor and patient relationship. The question of whether Article 2 of the European Convention on Human Rights (The Right to Life) is breached by the failure of English law to impose a duty upon individuals to assist is questionable.

## LEGAL CONSEQUENCES OF PROLONGING LIFE

Although they cannot legally be taken into account when deciding whether or not to do so, the ability to artificially prolong life may have legal consequences other than the criminal. For example, it can alter rights of inheritance in a particular case, it may alter pension entitlements or the amount of income or inheritance tax payable if life is prolonged into a new tax year in which rates or allowances are changed and it can affect the size of the damages in road traffic accident cases.

$$\boxed{2}$$

# Certifying the Death

## THE DOCTOR'S CERTIFICATE

If the death takes place in hospital or in a nursing home, the hospital or home will arrange the issue of a doctor's certificate confirming death and its cause.

The certificate is given in a sealed envelope and must be issued before the funeral can be arranged or the death registered with the Registrar of Births, Deaths and Marriages. The doctor will also give another certificate which explains the procedure to register the death and confirms that the certificate confirming death has been given. The first doctor's certificate must be taken to the registrar unopened within five days of being issued or within 42 days in the case of a stillbirth. A stillbirth is the birth of a baby who is born dead after the 24th week of pregnancy. A stillborn baby can be named and the stillbirth must be registered. A certificate for burial or cremation of a stillborn baby must be obtained from the registrar before its funeral can take place.

When death occurs at home, the patient's own doctor should be called. He will issue the certificates unless he has not seen the person who has died and who is called the deceased within the previous 14 days, in which case he will have to report the death to the coroner.

## CORONERS

The coroner is a lawyer or a doctor and sometimes both!

In the following additional cases the death will be reported to the coroner:

◆ accidental death;

◆ sudden unexpected death;

◆ where the cause of death is uncertain;

◆ if the death is thought to be the result of industrial disease;

◆ violent death;

◆ when death occurred in suspicious circumstances;

◆ death in the custody of the police or prison authorities;

◆ death during the course of an operation or before recovery from the anaesthetic.

The coroner's powers to enquire into deaths within his jurisdiction also applies to deaths abroad, at sea or in the air, if the body is brought into the coroner's area, for example by a ship bringing the body into an harbour within his area.

Under sections 271–273 of the Merchant Shipping Act 1995, in cases where:

- death occurs on a British ship; or

- the master of a British ship dies outside the United kingdom; or

- the death of a seaman occurs outside the United Kingdom as a result of injury or disease suffered while or within one year of serving on a British ship; then

unless a coroner's inquest is to be held, an enquiry must be held by the superintendent or proper officer of the next port at which the ship calls and a copy of the report of the enquiry will be given, upon request, to the next of kin or any person whom the Secretary of State considers to have a valid interest in it. This provision can prove useful in appropriate circumstances if a claim for compensation is contemplated.

If the death is reported to the coroner, certificates to enable the death to be registered and to authorise a funeral to take place will be issued by the coroner and not by the doctor, but not until a post mortem examination of the body and possibly an inquest has taken place. This applies whether or not the death takes place at home, in a nursing home or in a hospital.

A post mortem is an examination of the body by a pathologist. Relatives have the right to choose a doctor to represent them at the post mortem.

## INQUESTS
In the following cases the coroner will hold an inquest:

- if after the post mortem examination the cause of death remains uncertain;

- if the death appears to have been an unnatural or a violent one;

- where the death occurred in prison;

- when the death appears to have been caused by a reportable industrial disease.

The coroner holds the inquest in public and its sole purpose is to ascertain the cause and circumstances of death. Its purpose is not to apportion blame. There is a legal right for relatives of the deceased to attend the inquest if they wish and to ask questions relevant to the circumstances and cause of death. There is no right for anyone to make speeches. Relatives of the deceased also have the right to be represented by a lawyer, but legal aid is not granted for the purpose of representation at inquests. It is wise to be legally represented at an inquest if claims by the deceased's estate for compensation following from the circumstances of the death are likely.

In holding an inquest a coroner is conducting a hearing in a court of law and although proceedings are kept fairly informal the coroner has power to compel witnesses to attend and takes evidence on oath. Sometimes the coroner will have a jury to assist him in coming to his conclusion or verdict as to the identity of the deceased and the cause of death. The coroner's verdict does not preclude further proceedings in the civil or criminal courts.

If the death is one which should be reported to a coroner, the coroner's consent will be required before the body can be used for organ transplants or other medical purposes.

If the body is to be used for medical research, ask the medical attendant to make the necessary arrangements or contact the Inspector of Anatomy at the Anatomy Office of the nearest teaching hospital. In case of difficulty telephone HM Inspector of Anatomy on 020 7972 4342. A hospital is not obliged to accept a body for teaching purposes and it will not be accepted if unsuitable, for example if a post mortem has taken place. If accepted for teaching purposes, the body might be kept for up to three years.

If it is intended that parts of the body shall be used for an organ transplant, it is essential that the medical attendant be informed as soon as possible because the organs will be of no value if they are not removed promptly.

If tissue from the body is to be donated for research it must similarly be removed promptly. A tissue bank is maintained by the Histology Department of the Peterborough District Hospital which will collect and return bodies within a 150-mile radius. They are usually kept for about 24 hours and the tissue is used for research into pharmaceutical products. This might appeal to those who object to the testing of drugs on animals.

(3)

# Registering the Death

When the doctor's certificate, or if appropriate the coroner's certificate, as to the cause of death has been obtained, it is necessary to register the death with a Registrar of Births, Deaths and Marriages within five days, or in the case of a stillbirth, within 42 days. The particulars for registration may be given to any registrar who will forward them to the registrar for the subdistrict in which the death took place, where it will be officially registered.

The addresses of the registrars can be obtained from the local telephone book, local council, the doctor, hospital or nursing home.

Some registrars require an appointment to be made to save waiting, so it is a good idea to telephone first.

## THE PARTICULARS REQUIRED
The information which is required to be given is the full names and addresses of the person registering the death and of the person who has died (including the maiden name of the deceased in the case of a woman), the date and place of birth of the deceased, his occupation and last usual address, the date of the death and the location

where it took place, and particulars of any allowance or pension which the deceased was receiving from public funds. If the deceased was married the person registering the death will also be required to state the full name, occupation and date of birth of the surviving spouse. The doctor's or coroner's certificates as to the cause of death will have to be handed to the registrar unless the coroner has sent his certificate direct, so remember to take along all the information, the deceased's medical card and the certificates.

If the particulars are given to the registrar for the subdistrict in which the death took place, the registrar will give to the person supplying the information a registrar's death certificate and ask if any official copies of the certificate are required. There is a fee for the certificate and for each copy, but it is cheaper if copies are obtained when registering the death than if they are obtained later. Some copies will be needed to avoid delay later. I suggest that a copy for each relative who has the deceased's life insured and three copies in addition to the original of the registrar's copy is a sensible practical number. The fee is currently £3.50 for each copy if acquired when registering the death and £6.50 for each copy acquired later.

The Registrar will also supply a free certificate of registration of death (form BD8), usable only for Social Security purposes.

Unless the coroner has been involved and issued one, the registrar will also give a certificate (known as the Green

Form) authorising the funeral to take place. If an inquest is lengthy it is sometimes possible to obtain an Order for Burial (form 101) or a certificate for cremation from the coroner before the conclusion of the inquest, if he is satisfied that the body is no longer required.

If the particulars are given to the registrar of a subdistrict other than the one in which the death took place, the certificates will be sent by post.

## DEATHS ABROAD

Although there is no statutory requirement to register the death in England or Wales if the death takes place on a foreign registered ship or aircraft or abroad (which for this purpose includes in Scotland, Northern and Southern Ireland) the death should be registered (a) with the British Consulate and (b) in accordance with the law and procedures of the country concerned.

Registration of the death with the British Consulate enables one to obtain copies of the death certificate from the consulate or from the Overseas Registration Section, Smedleys Hydro, Trafalgar Road, Birkdale, Southport PR8 2HH.

If the death takes place out of the United Kingdom the British Consulate will be prepared to help with advice on the formalities for registering the death abroad and the procedures involved in returning the body to the United Kingdom.

# Arranging the Funeral

The funeral can take place as soon as is desired after the issue of the certificate for burial or cremation or it can be delayed for a reasonable period to suit the family. It is not legally necessary to have a religious ceremony or indeed any funeral ceremony, although it is unusual not to. It is legally necessary to dispose of the body, which cannot just be left. Although it is the executor's duty and right to arrange the funeral, in practice the family usually arranges it. If there is no one able and willing to arrange a funeral, the local authority will step in and arrange a basic funeral.

If the funeral is for a stillborn child (whether born at home or in hospital), the local hospital will usually be prepared to provide a free funeral. Maternity benefits may also be payable in cases of a stillbirth as well as in the case of a live birth.

The deceased may have left instructions in or with a will or spoken with family or friends as regards a preference for burial or cremation and as regards the form of the funeral. While the decision of any executor with regard to these matters is final (unless the law itself has required burial instead of cremation), it is usual to honour the deceased's wishes. The law will not forbid cremation unless there has been a suspicion of foul play.

If it is intended to take a body out of England and Wales (for example for a funeral), the coroner's permission must be obtained whether or not it has been necessary to report the death to the coroner.

## BRINGING A BODY BACK FROM ABROAD

The body of a person who has died on a foreign ship or aircraft or out of England or Wales ('abroad') can be brought back to England or Wales for a funeral, but it is expensive to do so and a death certificate and authority to return the body will have to be obtained from the relevant foreign country.

The circumstances in which it is necessary to report a death to the coroner in the case of a death within his area in England and Wales also make it necessary to report the death to the coroner if the body is brought within his area from abroad.

Before the funeral of a person who died abroad can be arranged in England or Wales it is necessary to obtain a Certificate of No Liability to Register the death from the registrar of the subdistrict in which it is proposed that the funeral shall take place, unless a coroner's authority for burial or cremation has been obtained. If the funeral is to be a cremation, either authority from the Coroners Section the Home Office or (if the death is not the result of natural causes) a certificate for cremation from the coroner is also required. It is also necessary to produce an authenticated translation of the foreign death certificate which shows the cause of death.

## ALTERNATIVE FUNERAL ARRANGEMENTS

A funeral can be arranged and carried out with or without the assistance of a funeral director.

### HIV/AIDS

Although AIDS and HIV are not diseases which are notifiable under the Public Health Act 1984, the Public Health (Infectious Diseases) Regulations 1998 (SI 1998 No. 1546) applies sections 43 and 44 of the act to AIDS and HIV.

Section 43 authorises a local authority or doctor to prevent the removal of the body of a person who has died from AIDS from hospital except direct to a mortuary or for burial or cremation and section 44 imposes a duty upon a person in whose house a person has died from AIDS to take reasonably practical steps to prevent anyone coming into contact with the body unnecessarily. Breaches of these provisions are backed by criminal sanctions but in practice they are seldom enforced.

In cases of death following HIV or AIDS advice can be obtained from FACTS Health Centre, the Terrence Higgins Trust or the London Lighthouse Trust.

### Muslim funerals

The Muslim Burial Council of Leicestershire will give advice about arranging a Muslim funeral.

## 'Green' and 'DIY' burials

Some people prefer to have a 'green' funeral and advice on arranging a 'green', 'woodland' or 'DIY' funeral can be obtained from the Natural Death Centre, a non-profit-making charity. The centre publishes information and is prepared to e-mail information and advice on the subject. Its principal publication, *The New Natural Death Handbook*, is a source of information as to such matters as available woodland burial sites and suppliers of funeral goods such as urns, shrouds and cardboard or traditional coffins by overnight mail order.

Although burial does not have to take place in a churchyard or cemetery, it must not constitute a danger to public health or pose a pollution threat to the water supply and it is as well to check first that the local authority has no objection. If it is proposed to carry out the burial in the garden of the deceased's home careful thought should be given to the resale value of the property and the problem of tending the grave if the property is sold at a future date. To bury a body on another person's land without their permission would be illegal as constituting a trespass to the land. Whenever a burial takes place on private land, it is wise to check the title deeds to ensure that they do not contain restrictions on the use of the land which prevent the use of the land for burial purposes. It is also wise to keep a record of the site of the burial with the title deeds because it is illegal to disturb a grave without permission from the Home Office. The date and place of the burial must be notified to the Registrar of Deaths within 96 hours of the burial.

A burial must not disturb a recognised archaeological site and any grave marker, high fencing or wall or multiple burials might require planning permission.

### Burial at sea

Burial at sea is better arranged with the assistance of a professional funeral director. A licence from the Department of the Environment, Farming and Rural Affairs and a special coffin are required. It can only take place in certain parts of the sea and the coroner's permission is required to take the body out of the country. Such burials are expensive.

### Cremation

A cremation can only take place at an authorised crematorium but ashes can be buried on one's own private land, on the land of another with the owner's permission or scattered at sea.

## FUNERALS WITH THE AID OF A PROFESSIONAL FUNERAL DIRECTOR

To arrange a funeral with the assistance of a professional funeral director, take the registrar's copy of the death certificate and either the registrar's or the coroner's certificate for burial or cremation to the funeral director. If the deceased died abroad the Certificate of No Liability to Register and the authority from the Home Office, if applicable, should also be taken to the director. Agree the arrangements (place, time, burial or cremation, type of coffin, number of cars, minister to officiate at the ceremony, etc.) with the undertaker. Check that the proposed burial ground is not likely to object to the type of headstone or other memorial that you have in mind because churches and municipal cemetery proprietors are becoming increasingly particular as to what they will allow. Although it seems tasteless at such a time, one should get a quotation from the undertaker as to the cost and one can even shop around if one feels so inclined!

The undertaker can arrange publication of any death notices that might be desired, any donations to a favourite charity and floral tributes, or you can arrange these yourself or dispense with them. Floral tributes may be sent direct to the undertakers or to the place where the principal mourners will meet on the day of the funeral. If cremation has been decided upon, at many crematoria the floral tributes will be disposed of after a few hours and one might prefer to give instructions that cut flowers go to a local hospital instead.

In the case of cremation it will usually be necessary to decide what is to be done with the ashes but in the case of babies there may be no ashes.

If there is to be a religious ceremony the officiating minister will arrange a meeting to ascertain information for his eulogy about the person who has died and to discuss anything required by the family or the deceased as to the form of the service, e.g. music, readings, any lying in church or requiem mass, etc. Friends and relatives may be invited to speak at the ceremony and should be notified of the date, time and place of the funeral. One should try to ascertain how many will attend the funeral and require transport to the church and how many will stay for refreshments after the funeral. It is usual to issue a general invitation to those attending the funeral (or at least to ask the closest friends and relatives attending) to return to the house or to repair to a local restaurant or pub for light refreshments. Some of those attending may have put themselves out or travelled a long way to attend.

# (5)

# The Funeral

The hearse and additional cars arrive at the place where the principal mourners have met (usually the deceased's house or a relative's house) and the mourners leave the house led by the chief mourners, who are usually the nearest relatives. If there is to be a ceremony the chief mourners lead the other mourners into the church or crematorium chapel following the coffin and sit on the front row. After the ceremony mourners follow the coffin to the grave if there is a burial and after the burial (or after the ceremony if a cremation and not a burial is involved) the chief mourners stop for a few minutes to thank the other mourners for attending and then all are free to leave.

It has been known for burglars to scan the press for details of forthcoming funerals and it is sometimes arranged for 'house-sitters' to stay in the house while the funeral takes place, to ensure that refreshments are ready and to welcome the mourners when they return.

## DEALING WITH COMPLAINTS

If there is a complaint against the funeral director which cannot be resolved directly with him, try contacting the local authority's Trading Standards Department. If it proves impossible to resolve a complaint against a funeral director which cannot be resolved directly with him, try contacting the local authority's Trading Standards Department. If it proves impossible to resolve a complaint against a funeral director who is a member of a trade association's conciliation scheme might be of assistance. If all else fails one can always seek redress in the local small claims court.

## MEETING THE COSTS OF THE FUNERAL

The person who arranges the funeral is contractually liable to pay the bill, but an executor or the administrator of an estate who pays for the funeral has a legal right to be reimbursed by the estate if the deceased's estate is sufficient to cover the cost. If there is no one able or willing to meet the cost of the funeral, the local authority or, if the deceased died in hospital, the local health authority for the area in which the deceased died will arrange the funeral. If the health authority or local authority arrange and pay for the funeral they also have a right to reimbursement from the estate.

### Existing grave space

A search through the deceased's papers might produce a deed of grave space showing that space in an existing grave or a new grave has already been paid for but remember that the cost of the funeral is more than the cost of a grave. A hearse, funeral cars, any minister and grave diggers, etc. all have to be paid for so, it is as well to get a quotation before entering into a commitment.

## Funeral prepayment plans

The deceased may have made arrangements for payment of the cost of the funeral to be made from a funeral prepayment plan and some occupational pension schemes, professional bodies, provident clubs and trade unions might make a payment towards funeral costs.

## Membership of the Cremation Society or private crematoria

Shareholders in certain funeral companies and private crematoria sometimes get a reduction in the funeral costs and members of the Cremation Society are sometimes able to claim a reduction in fees.

## Serving members of the armed forces

The Ministry of Defence will assist with the cost and type of funeral, the precise help given depending on the place of death, the type of funeral requested and the place where it is to take place.

## War pensioners

If the deceased was a war pensioner who fulfilled certain conditions, a non-repayable grant to help with the cost of a basic funeral is available. Enquiry should be made of the War Pensions Agency.

## The Social Fund

A partner or other person who reasonably assumed responsibility for a funeral in the absence of a partner or close relatives able to meet the cost, and who is receiving certain means tested benefits, can sometimes obtain a contribution from the Social Fund. Application must be made to the Benefits Agency within three months of the date of the funeral.

**Bank and building society accounts and National Savings**
Unless the deceased had a joint bank account or the total value of the estate was less than £5,000, money in a clearing bank account will not normally be available to meet the cost of the funeral until a grant of probate of the will or letters of administration has been issued by a probate registry, but if there is pressure from the funeral director for payment, a building society account or National Savings investments can sometimes be used to pay the funeral bill before the grant has been issued. Enquiry should be made of the building society or the appropriate department of National Savings and Investments.

# Bereavement and Other Social Security Benefits

The death of your spouse will cause substantial changes in your financial situation and may give you entitlement to new social security benefits or affect existing benefits.

Both men and women whose husbands or wives have died after 9 April 2001 may be able to claim bereavement benefits which depend on individual circumstances.

## BEREAVEMENT PAYMENT AND BEREAVEMENT ALLOWANCE

◆ **Bereavement Payment**. You may be entitled to a single tax-free payment known as a Bereavement Payment which is based on your spouse's National Insurance contributions, if your spouse was not entitled to a state retirement pension when he or she died or you are under pensionable age, but the claim for Bereavement Payment must be made within three months of the death unless there are exceptional circumstances.

◆ **Bereavement Allowance**. You may be entitled to a periodic payment known as a Bereavement Allowance for up to 52 weeks or until you reach pensionable age, whichever period is the shorter. The amount of the payment is based in part upon your spouse's National Insurance contributions and in part upon your age when your spouse dies. You must be aged at least 45 when your spouse dies to make a successful claim. The claim should be made promptly because the allowance will only be payable from the date of the claim and not from the date of the death if claimed after three months from the date of the death.

Even if your spouse had made insufficient National Insurance contributions you may be able to claim Bereavement Payment and Bereavement Allowance if he or she died as the result of an industrial disease or accident.

There is one claim form for the above benefits which is obtainable from the local Benefits Agency, the address of which can be found in a telephone directory.

It must be remembered that Bereavement Payment and Bereavement Allowance are only payable in respect of those who were legally married at the time of the death (not partners) and that for benefit purposes, if you remarry or live with another as man and wife, you cease to be a widow or widower as the case may be.

Whether you are employed or not does not affect your entitlement to bereavement benefits.

## THE STATE RETIREMENT PENSION

If you are receiving the State Retirement Pension in your own right when your spouse dies, you may be entitled to an increase in the pension, and if you are not receiving a

State Retirement Pension, you may become entitled to one. In each case it depends upon your late spouse's contribution record. Enquire at the Benefits Office.

## WAR WIDOWS PENSION

War Widows Pension is becoming increasingly rare as the years pass, but if obtainable it is a particularly valuable benefit in that it is tax-free. It may be payable if your parent or husband was receiving certain benefits as a consequence of injuries received in a war or his death resulted from injuries suffered in war with H.M. armed forces.

## JOB SEEKER'S ALLOWANCE

After the bereavement you might feel that not only do you need more money but you also have more available time and are lonely. If you decide to seek work you should note that you might be able to claim Job Seeker's Allowance if you are over 18 and under pensionable age and you are capable of work which you are actively seeking and for which you are available. The benefit is claimable either on the basis of low income or National Insurance contributions.

## MINIMUM INCOME GUARANTEE AND INCOME SUPPORT

These are very similar means tested benefits for people aged 16 and over who are not working more than 16 hours a week. Income Support is for those under the age of 60 and Minimum Income Guarantee is for those aged 60 or over. These benefits may be increased to help with the cost of housing.

## SOCIAL FUND PAYMENTS

I have previously referred to assistance from the Social Fund with the cost of the funeral. Other grants and loans which do not depend upon National Insurance contributions are also available from the Social Fund to help with expenses which are burdensome and non-recurring. Some, but not all, are dependent upon already being in receipt of Income Support or income-based Job Seeker's Allowance and some, but not all, have to be repaid. Those which are loans and not grants and have to be repaid are free of interest.

## ASSISTANCE WITH CHILDREN

If you are left to care for a child or children enquire at the Benefits Office for other assistance which might be available for you.

## BENEFITS FROM LOCAL AUTHORITIES

In addition to the above benefits if you are on a low income and pay rent you might be entitled to Housing Benefit from the local council and if you are on a low income and pay council tax you might be entitled to Council Tax Benefit. These two benefits are means tested. Remember also that if the death leaves you living alone in your property you will be entitled to a reduction of 25 per cent on your council tax bill and the following people who may in fact be living with you are ignored for the purpose of deciding whether or not you are living alone:

♦ anyone under the age of 18;

♦ students and those in further education;

- student nurses;

- Youth Training trainees and apprentices;

- anyone who has severe mental problems;

- those other than partners who care for you if you have a disability and receive certain benefits;

- paid care workers who live in;

- members of the armed forces and certain international institutions.

# Part 2

# Winding up Money Matters

(7)

# Who Can and Should Wind Up Money Matters?

When a person dies it is necessary for someone to wind up that person's estate, i.e. their money, possessions, property and debts, by collecting what is due to the deceased, paying the debts including any inheritance tax and passing anything that remains to those entitled to it.

## EXECUTORS

Who is entitled to wind up the estate depends upon whether or not the deceased has left a will or codicil appointing an executor who is still living. A codicil is a document separate from the will but which is similarly signed and completed and which adds to or amends the will. An executor is a person to whom the will or codicil gives the task of carrying out the will.

If the deceased left a will, the people with the first right to deal with or administering the estate are the executors appointed by the will, but if the appointed sole executor is under the age of 18, he cannot act, although the High Court can appoint his parent, guardian or another person to act for him until he becomes of age.

Even though a person has been named in a will as an executor, he is not obliged to act as executor. He can sign a form of renunciation (obtainable from law stationers) giving up the right to the executorship, provided that he does so before he exercises any of the rights or carries out any of the duties of an executor. If one appointed executor renounces executorship, the other appointed executors may proceed to obtain a grant of probate of the will.

A further possibility is for an appointed executor to ask the probate registry to allow the other executors to go ahead and prove the will without him, without finally giving up his right to act as executor at a later stage should he later wish to do so. This is known as reserving power to prove a will and is particularly useful to cover the possibility that one of two executors might obtain probate alone but die before completing the winding up of the estate. The executor to whom probate has been reserved can then apply to the probate registry for authority to take over and finalise the administration and the winding up of the estate.

If all the executors are unable or unwilling to take on the work or the will has not given anyone the position of executor, the person entitled to wind up the estate is the person to whom the deceased has left the entirety of his estate. If there is no such person, the person entitled to wind up the estate is the person to whom the will leaves that part of the estate which remains after taking out any gifts or legacies made by the will. If there is no such person again, there is a set order of precedence for other people entitled to deal with the estate ending with the Crown, but the list is so complex as to be outside the scope of this book.

## WHERE THERE IS NO WILL

If no will has been made, the persons entitled to wind up the estate are the following persons, with priority being given to each group in the order in which each group is described below:

1. Husband or wife

2. Sons or daughters or their decendants

3. Parents

4. Brothers or sisters of the whole blood or their descendants

5. Brothers or sisters of the half blood or their descendants

6. Grandparents

7. Uncles or aunts of the whole blood or their descendants

8. Uncles or aunts of the half blood or their descendants

9. The Crown

10. Creditors of the deceased.

All those within each group are equally entitled.

## GRANT OF REPRESENTATION

To prove a right to wind up an estate one obtains, i.e. 'takes out' from a probate registry, a document called **probate** if one is an executor appointed by the will or **letters of administration of the estate** in any other case. Both probate and letters of administration are sometimes referred to as the grant of representation.

Any number up to four of the people within each group specified above or any four executors may take out the grant together, but people from different groups may not be mixed.

To have entitlement to wind up an estate a person must also be of full age and of sound mind.

## SHOULD ONE EMPLOY A SOLICITOR?

Each course has its advantages and disadvantages.

The main advantages of employing a solicitor are:

- ◆ If the terms of the will are contentious or not clear, the solicitor who is trained in the law and experienced in these matters should be able to give sound guidance.

- ◆ In the event of a mistake being made as a result of his negligence, the solicitor will be insured to cover any claims by the executor or the beneficiaries including the cost of properly pursuing such claims.

- ◆ Much of the burden of the routine work involved will be taken over by the solicitor, although it will still be necessary for the personal representative to spend a great deal of time searching out documents, having meetings with and writing letters to the solicitor, signing authorities, receipts and withdrawal forms, etc.

◆ If the personal representative is a close friend or relative of the deceased, everything the personal representative does in relation to the estate will be a reminder and perhaps prove upsetting.

The main advantage of the DIY approach is:

◆ Cost saving – solicitors' businesses are expensive to run and, as most people will know, their fees are not cheap, although few who have not experienced employing a solicitor in a probate matter will realise how expensive this can be.

Let me explain by way of an example.

The usual practice in probate matters is for a solicitor to charge a fee based on the time spent in carrying out the work, the fee being known as the hourly rate (i.e. charge per hour). Frequently, in addition, a solicitor will charge fees based on a percentage of the gross estate.

The hourly rate depends upon the individual solicitor's proportion of the cost of running the practice and the seniority of the person doing the work. Typical hourly rates at the present time might be between £75 and £200.

The percentage charge is usually ½ per cent of the value of any freehold property involved and 1 per cent of the remainder of the estate. These percentages are frequently increased by one half if the solicitor is also the executor.

Even more might be charged if unusually complex legal points arise.

Therefore, suppose someone dies leaving an estate consisting of, say:

♦ a freehold house valued at £180,000;

♦ furniture and personal effects of £15,000;

♦ life insurance policies £10,000;

♦ balance at the bank £300;

♦ savings with a two building societies totalling £8,000;

♦ an ISA value £12,000;

♦ Premium Bonds £700;

♦ Pensioners Bonds £2,000;

♦ cash £100;

♦ de-mutualisation and privatisation shares made up of four different holdings totalling £5,900.

Suppose also there are three beneficiaries and two non-professional executors. A solicitor's fee for the work to be done would probably be calculated as follows:

Percentage charge on the house (½% of
 £180,000)                                            £900.00

| | |
|---|---|
| Percentage charge on the remainder of the estate | £540.00 |
| Hourly rate charge: 14 hours at £100 per hour | £1,400.00 |
| Total fee exclusive of VAT | £2,840.00 |
| Add VAT at 17.5% of £2,840 | £497.00 |
| | |
| Total bill saved on this estate if no solicitor is employed | £3,337.00 |

If the solicitor is an executor his percentage rate would be increased as mentioned above and the total bill including VAT would be £4,183.00, and possibly higher if the solicitor is a partner.

◆ The personal representative is much more in control of the pace at which the winding up of the estate progresses and is fully aware of the situation at all times. Most solicitors work under great pressure and do not find the time to chase up a tardy reply. Unless carried out by someone who does no other work than probate work, the probate files tend to get put on one side and take second priority to court work and conveyancing where there are strict time limits with disastrous consequences if the time limits are not met. Moreover, most solicitors are notoriously bad at keeping the client informed of progress or lack of progress.

# Winding up an Estate Yourself

## JOINTLY OWNED PROPERTY

There are two ways of owning property jointly in English law, namely as joint tenants or as tenants in common. The use of the word 'tenants' has nothing to do with tenants in the sense of landlord and tenant: it is merely the same word used as a technical term to signify a different concept.

If people own property as joint tenants the law provides that on the death of one owner, that person's share is inherited by the surviving joint owners regardless of the terms of the deceased's will or the next of kin, but a share of property which is owned as tenants in common is inherited on death as provided in the deceased's will, if there is one, or if none, then by the next of kin in accordance with the intestacy laws.

It follows therefore that if property is owned as joint tenants, all that is necessary for the survivor to prove a right to deal with the property and to inherit it is to produce satisfactory evidence of death, i.e. a death certificate, or an order of a court giving leave to presume death.

On the other hand if property is owned as tenants in common, the person claiming the right to deal with the deceased's share as executor of a will must prove that he is the executor appointed by a valid will and if there is no will or a will but no executor appointed or willing to prove it, other proof must be given of the right to deal with the deceased's share of the jointly owned property.

The document evidencing proof that the will is a valid one is called probate of the will or, if the will has not appointed an executor who is willing to prove it or all the appointed executors have died before the person who made the will, it is called letters of administration.

If no valid will exists the next of kin must obtain a different document (also confusingly called letters of administration) to prove the right to deal with the deceased's assets including any share of jointly owned property which was held as tenants in common.

Grants of probate and letters of administration are sometimes conveniently referred to as the grant of representation and the way they are obtained is described on pages 71–75.

How does one know whether jointly owned property was held as joint tenants or tenants in common? Usually bank and building society accounts and stocks and shares are held in joint tenancies, but if there is any evidence to show that the joint owners owned separate shares of the property as opposed to each joint owner owning the entirety, the joint ownership is a case of tenancies in common. Joint tenants always own the asset equally and words indicating that the joint owners own unequally always mean a tenancy in common. Partnerships almost invariably own property as tenants in common. When husbands and wives own property jointly they usually, but not necessarily, do so as joint tenants and not tenants in common.

## IF THE GROSS ESTATE IS VALUED UNDER £5,000

If the value of the estate before deducting the cost of the funeral and any debts left by the deceased is under £5,000 it is frequently worth writing to the bodies which hold the assets to ask that they make payment to the personal representative without the necessity of going to the expense of obtaining a grant of representation and what their requirements are to enable this to be done.

Usually building societies and banks etc. will make payment in such circumstances to those entitled in return for sight of the original will, if any, or if there is no will, in return for a short statement as to the identity and relationship of the next of kin, and in each case the signature of a short form of indemnity which the bank or building society will prepare.

## IF THE GROSS ESTATE IS VALUED OVER £5,000

If the value of the estate before deducting the cost of the funeral and any debts left by the deceased is over £5,000, then before the assets of the estate can be dealt with, probate of the will or letters of administration must be obtained.

The procedure to be followed is essentially the same in the case of both probate and letters of administration.

There are three main steps involved:

1. obtaining the information necessary to prepare the papers to obtain the grant of representation;

2. preparing and lodging the documentation to obtain inheritance tax assessment and the issue of the grant of representation; and

3. registering the grant in connection with the various assets and giving instructions as to how they are to be dealt with, e.g. transferred to a person entitled on the death, sold or cashed and collecting what is due to the estate.

Following the completion of the above three steps to finally wind up the money side one must:

◆ finalise the income and capital gains tax positions;

◆ pay off the debts and discharge the liabilities of the estate; and

◆ distribute the remaining assets of the estate to those who are entitled to them (who are called the beneficiaries).

Each step is separately explained below and appendixes contain appropriate drafts for most of the letters that will need to be written and useful addresses.

## COLLECTING THE NECESSARY INFORMATION TO OBTAIN THE GRANT OF REPRESENTATION

It is useful to start by making a list of everything the deceased had which can be turned into money (whether or not sale is intended) and to list all the known debts. This list can be used as a worksheet and can be used to record information which will be required to prepare the papers which are necessary to obtain the grant of representation and to track progress in the administration of the estate, thus showing at a glance what has been done and what remains to be done at any time. An example of a suitable form of worksheet is set out in Appendix 1.

Sometimes it is difficult to discover exactly what assets a person leaves. If this is not known, a search of the home for papers will usually give clues. Besides safes and filing cabinets, many people use furniture drawers, bureaux and wardrobes to store (and hide!) their papers. I have even come across building society passbooks kept in the refrigerator (hot money?) and cash hidden on a ledge inside a disused fireplace, as well as cash under floorboards, carpets and a bed mattress. Safe and other keys are often hidden behind books on bookshelves.

Bank statements show direct payments into the account such as pension payments and share dividends. If a dividend has been received the company registrar will be able to confirm the holding. The registrar's address appears on the tax certificates attached to dividend warrants if any can be found. Do not forget that a company's website will also yield the company registrar's address. Sometimes the registrar's website will reveal the holding, although one will need the deceased's password to obtain details of the holding from the website.

Bank statements will also give a clue to regular outgoings.

If it is suspected there might be a bank or building society account but details are sparse, try completing and submitting a dormant account form obtainable from any bank or building society branch respectively.

Occupational and insured pension schemes must register and update their registered particulars annually under the pensions registry scheme. Following acquisitions, mergers and company insolvencies schemes may have changed their names. To trace suspected pension entitlements from former employers, try submitting a Pensions Trace Request Form (obtainable from some post offices or from the Registry) to the Registry of Pensions at the Occupational Pensions Board. The tracing service is free.

The British Bankers Association and the Building Societies Association may be able to help where there have been mergers, takeovers or changes in the names of member institutions.

National Savings and Investments runs a scheme to trace possible accounts, certificates and premium bond prizes and a National Savings Tracing Service application form can be obtained from Freepost BJ2092, Blackpool FY39XR, or by telephoning 0845 964 5000.

Since the Financial Services and Marketing Act 2000 came into force on 1 December 2001, the Financial Services Authority is responsible for regulating all deposit insurance and investment business in this country and has taken over a vast number of records. The Authority maintains a Register of Firms which can be very useful and might be able to help in tracing changes in friendly societies and insurance companies.

Enquiry can also be made of the deceased's solicitors, bank, accountant, stockbroker and other financial advisers for the required financial information and as to whether or not they have knowledge of a will. In addition to searching the places where other papers are usually found, enquiry can be made at Probate Registries for wills which are sometimes deposited there for safe-keeping. Even if one has found a will there could be later wills in existence.

Care should be taken to include only items that belong to the deceased in the estate and to exclude library items or NHS equipment such as wheelchairs, artificial aids or limbs which should be returned.

Television and motor car licences, season tickets and membership documents in respect of associations and clubs should be returned promptly in case it is possible to obtain a refund of fees.

When the list is more or less complete, steps should be taken to obtain a figure for the value of each asset and the amount of each debt or other liability and the appropriate figure should be entered on the list. A value as at the date of death must be obtained for every asset and liability of the estate before a grant of representation to the estate can be obtained. The value required for inheritance tax purposes and to obtain a grant of representation to an estate is the open market value as at the date of death, i.e. the price that the item could reasonably be expected to obtain if sold on the open market as at the date of death. If the death occurred on a non-trading day such as a Sunday, the lower of the preceding or next trading days may be used.

### Bank and building society accounts

Each bank or building society should be written to at an early stage with a copy of the death certificate and most will also require sight of the original or a photostat copy of the will. A statement of the balance standing to the credit of each account including accrued interest as at the date of death should be obtained and if there is a passbook it should be enclosed to be made up to date.

The addresses can usually be obtained from the passbooks (if any), from old account statements, telephone directories, or on the society's website on the Internet.

The bank or building society will freeze the account and stop making standing orders and meeting direct debits when notified of the death.

### Employment benefits

If the deceased was in employment at the date of death the employer should be written to in order to ascertain whether there are arrears of wages or any other benefits due to the estate at the date of death. The employer should also be asked to give useful information such as the address of the relevant tax district and tax reference of the deceased and the same information as to any pension scheme trustees. The trustees of the pension scheme should be asked to supply information as to whether there are any, and if so what, benefits due from the pension scheme and whether such benefits fall to be included in the estate for inheritance tax purposes.

If the deceased had changed employment or retired and there is difficulty in tracing the trustees of a pension scheme the Pension Schemes Registry might be able to help.

**Furniture and personal effects**
Items of furniture and personal effects need not be individually valued and usually a fair estimate of their total value is sufficient, but a professional valuation should be obtained from an auctioneer or valuer if they are not the usual run-of-the-mill items and it is suspected that they may be of significant value.

**PEPs, ISAs TESSAs and unit trusts**
The managers of PEPs, ISAs, TESSAs and any unit trust holding must be written to for a valuation of the holding as at the date of death unless the valuation can be obtained from prices quoted in the press.

If the death occurred on a non-trading day such as a Sunday, the lower of the preceding or next trading days can be used.

Unit trusts, unlike OEICS (open-ended investment company shares), have two prices: one at which the manager is prepared to sell the units and a lower price at which he is prepared to buy back the units. Unit trusts are valued for inheritance tax and probate purposes at the lower of the two prices.

**Stocks and shares quoted on a recognised stock exchange**
Likewise stocks and shares have two prices – a buying price and a selling price – and if the death occurred on a non-trading day such as a Sunday, the lower of the preceding or next trading days may be used.

The price quoted in the press as the closing price on any day is usually a middle price, half way between the closing buying and selling prices.

The proper way of valuing stocks and shares for inheritance tax and probate purposes is to work out two figures and to use the lower figure. The first figure is obtained by adding to the lower closing price a quarter of the difference between the buying and the selling price. The second figure is the average of the price of all recorded bargains for the day. The Stock Exchange Daily Official List for the relevant day gives closing prices of securities quoted on the London Stock Exchange and it can be consulted in some public library reference departments or purchased via FT Information Services or the publication section of The London Stock Exchange. Alternatively most stockbrokers or a bank will supply a valuation of a list of stocks or shares for probate purposes, but they do charge for the service and it might be wise to ask for an indication of the likely fee in advance.

If a share is quoted 'ex dividend', the dividend which has been declared must be included in the inheritance tax valuation of the estate: if loan or debenture stock is quoted ex interest then the interest less tax at the appropriate rate (currently 20 per cent) must be included.

## Unquoted stocks and shares

Any securities such as shares or loan or debenture stock which are not quoted on a recognised stock exchange are valued according to the percentage of the company's share capital held by the deceased. Thus a shareholding of 50 per cent or less is valued on the basis of the dividend yield, a holding of between 50 per cent and 90 per cent is valued on the basis of earnings yield and a holding of over 90 per cent upon an assets basis. The value will eventually have to be agreed by the Inland Revenue Shares Valuation Division, but the easiest way for the layman to get an initial figure is to ask the company secretary for a figure or if the deceased owned only a small percentage of the company's shares, to ask the secretary at what price dealings, if any, last took place and to use that price.

## Life and endowment policies

For these policies, write to the company concerned and try to deal with head office rather than the local office. The head office address usually appears on the policy document, but it might not be the latest address and the company name may have changed. In that event it might be necessary to visit the company's website or, if the name has changed, to enquire of the Financial Services Authority or the British Insurance Association.

The value of a policy which matures on the death of the deceased is the amount paid out by the assurance company. If the policy is one that matures on the death of another person, the inheritance tax value is what it can be sold for, i.e. its open market value, and not its surrender value which will usually be less.

If the policy was taken out by another person on the life of the deceased or taken out by the deceased expressly upon trust for another person, it will not form part of the deceased's estate and the insurance company will make payment to the person who took it out, or upon whose behalf it was taken out, as the case may be, upon production of the policy and a death certificate without the necessity of waiting for a grant of representation to be obtained.

### National Savings products

Government stock on the old National Savings Bank Register (now the Bank of England Register) is valued on the same basis as other stock exchange quoted stock or quoted shares.

Valuations for other National Savings products can be obtained by writing to the Director of Savings at the address for the relevant product given in Appendix 2.

### Benefits from the State

If the deceased was in receipt of any such benefit, e.g. unemployment, retirement or widow's benefit or income support, the Benefits Agency should be contacted quoting the deceased's National Insurance number and the position as to any arrears or overpaid benefit established. The address of the Benefits Agency can be obtained from the local telephone directory.

### Land and buildings

For houses and other land or buildings, talk to a local estate agent who might be prepared to give an opinion of the value for probate purposes, especially if he thinks that it might lead to a sale. Again ask if there will be a charge and if so how much. Do not ask for a formal valuation, which could be very expensive indeed, but for an opinion of the market price current as at the date of death.

As a last resort, ask yourself at what price you would have been prepared to sell the property.

Valuations for probate should be an accurate representation of the open market sale price as at the date of death because they will have to be sworn to by the personal representative, but when all is said and done, values are a matter of opinion unless the matter is tested by an actual sale and opinions differ.

If the Revenue disagrees with the personal representative's valuation, he can always concede gracefully to the Revenue's superior and better informed opinion and no harm will have been done, as long as the value originally suggested was not so far out as to be viewed as an obvious attempt to defraud the Revenue. If the Revenue does not challenge, a goodly sum of money might be saved by a fair and knowledgeable amateur valuation! If the Revenue do challenge the valuation and the personal representative cannot agree the Revenue's valuation, an appeal can be made to the Lands Tribunal or on a point of law to the High Court, but such appeals are costly and might well be unsuccessful. The Inland Revenue Stamp Duty Office informs the Local District Valuer of the price at which every sale in the Valuer's district takes place and so the District Valuer is well informed on such matters.

If the land or buildings are mortgaged, the full value should be included and the amount outstanding on the mortgage should be included separately as a liability of the estate. The mortgage might be supported by a whole life or endowment policy lodged as collateral security for the mortgage debt, in which case a value for the policy will also have to be obtained and the policy proceeds included in the probate papers as a separate asset.

**Interests in trusts**
If the deceased was entitled to income from a trust, the proportion of the value of the trust's assets, assessed in the same fraction as the income to which the deceased was entitled bears to the entire income of the trust, is included in the deceased's estate for inheritance tax purposes. Thus if the deceased was entitled to one quarter of the income of the trust, then one quarter of the value of the trust's assets (valued as described above) must be included in the value of the deceased's estate, even if the deceased was only entitled to that income during his lifetime.

## Income and capital gains taxes

The Inspector of Taxes who dealt with the deceased's tax matters should be notified of the death and enquiry should be made as to the standing of the deceased's tax affairs to ascertain the amount of tax outstanding or refunds of overpaid tax due to the estate.

Which tax office is the appropriate tax office depends upon the particular circumstances of the deceased. If the deceased had a pension from a former employer or was employed when he died, the pension payer or the employer will be able to supply the name and address of the relevant tax district and the tax reference: if the deceased was self employed, try the tax office nearest to the main place of business, and if the deceased was not in employment and had no occupational pension, contact the tax office closest to the home address. The addresses of tax offices can be found in telephone directories under Inland Revenue.

It will be necessary to complete final tax returns up to the date of death. It should also be mentioned at this stage that, before finally distributing the estate between those entitled to it, it will also be necessary to complete final tax returns and settle any outstanding tax due in relation to income received between death and final distribution. If the period of administration covers several tax years, a separate return will be required for each tax year or part of a tax year. Income received in respect of a period up to and after the date of death is not apportioned; which tax return it is entered into depends upon the date it is paid or due to be paid and not the period over which it accrues. It should be noted that no capital gains tax liability arises by reason of the death as opposed to liability for tax on gains arising on disposals by the deceased during his lifetime. Capital losses incurred by the deceased during his lifetime but in the year of his death may be carried back and set against net gains made in the three tax years preceding the tax year in which the deceased died. For capital gains tax purposes the beneficiaries of an estate are deemed to acquire assets transferred to them at their value as at the date of death.

### Debts and liabilities

If the deceased was in receipt of a pension (either state or private) or National Insurance benefits, the payers should be written to with a copy of the death certificate to enquire as to any sums underpaid or overpaid and repayable. Underpayments must be included in the documents to be prepared to lead to the issue of the grant of representation as assets of the estate and overpayments may be included as debts and deducted from the value of the estate for inheritance tax purposes, thus reducing the amount of any inheritance tax which will have to be paid.

Any mortgagees should be notified of the death promptly, as should the local authority for local government tax purposes, the suppliers of meals on wheels, any carers, the suppliers of gas, electricity, telephone, cable or satellite TV services and any body with which the deceased had credit cards. They should each be asked for the amount due to the date of death and they and all other known creditors should be requested to withhold any action contemplated to recover the debts until a grant of representation can be obtained and the estate put in funds.

If one-third of the purchase price of goods on hire purchase has been paid they cannot be repossessed without a court order.

In the case of credit cards, if the beneficiaries of the estate have the requisite funds, they may wish to pay off any outstanding funds to avoid interest charges accruing.

If the proposed personal representatives are not also the sole beneficiaries of the estate and are not sure that they know of all the debts, or are not certain that the deceased did not make a later will, or if they are not sure that they know all the relatives, they may wish to protect themselves by publishing a statutory advertisement for creditors pursuant to section 27 of the Trustee Act 1925. The advertisement should be published in *The London Gazette* and in a newspaper circulating in the area in which the deceased had a house or other land or lived. The broad effect of the publication of such notices is that anyone who reads the notice, but does not notify the personal representatives of a claim within two months of publication of the notice, is barred from claiming a debt or an entitlement under any later will or upon intestacy from the personal representatives after the estate has been distributed, unless the proposed representatives had notice of the debt from other sources. However, such claimants can still recover the debt from the beneficiaries.

A suitable form of notice appears in Appendix 1 and it should be noted that although local newspapers will usually accept such notices for publication before a grant of representation has been issued, the *London Gazette* has its own form of notice and will not accept the notice for publication from private individuals until a grant of representation is to hand.

## PREPARING AND LODGING THE DOCUMENTATION

The forms which have to be completed to obtain a grant of representation to the estate can be obtained from the Personal Applications Section of the Probate Registry or downloaded from the Court Service website. There are local probate offices in different parts of the country but in the event of difficulty write to:

Probate Department
The Principal Registry
Family Division
First Avenue House
42–49 High Holborn
London WC1V 6NP

With the forms the Probate Registry will usually send a brief guide on how to complete them and a note of what is to be returned with them. There should be no difficulty in completing the forms if the procedures outlined above have been followed and the relevant information obtained. When the forms have been filled in and signed by those applying for the grant, the forms should be returned to the registry with one of the copy death certificates obtained when registering the death and the originals of any will and codicils.

It is of the utmost importance to note that under no circumstances should anything ever be attached to the will in any way, even with a paperclip.

It is wise to keep a photostat copy of any will or codicil and it might also be useful to keep a photostat of any other documents sent to the Probate Registry, if this can be done without too much inconvenience.

After the registry has read the documents, the applicants for the grant will be invited to attend at the registry or a local probate office of their choice, by appointment, to affirm or swear on oath that the information which they have given is true. The attendance at the registry also gives the applicants and the registry an opportunity to deal with any matters which need to be clarified on either side. When the applicants attend the registry they are told the amount of the fee that has to be paid to the registry before the grant will be given out. Any inheritance tax payable will also have to be paid before the grant will be given to the personal representative. The registry's fee and the amount of inheritance tax depend upon the value of the estate involved.

If the personal representatives do not have sufficient, or indeed any, money to pay the inheritance tax and the registry's fee, but the estate includes National Savings Certificates, or SAYE contracts, or government stock on the Bank of England Register, or capital, deposit, children's, bonus, first option, pensioners guaranteed income, premium savings, or income bonds, the registry can arrange for these assets to be used towards payment of the tax and fees and the applicants should request this at interview with the registry.

Similarly, if the deceased had certificates of tax deposits, i.e. money on deposit with the Inland Revenue to meet future tax liabilities, that money can be used to pay inheritance tax before the grant of representation is issued.

If the deceased had money on deposit with a building society or bank, the building society or bank will usually allow as much of that money as is necessary to be used before probate for payment of inheritance tax.

Sometimes stockbrokers will arrange for securities held by the deceased in their nominee accounts to be used to pay inheritance tax and probate fees but this is not possible if the securities are held in certificated form and not in the broker's nominee account.

If there is no money or insufficient money on deposit to pay the tax, a society or bank will usually grant a loan at interest for that purpose and such interest is of course borne by the deceased's estate and not by the applicants for the grant personally. Interest on the loan should kept separately identifiable from interest on a loan obtained for any other purpose so that the interest on the loan for probate fees and/or inheritance tax can be deducted for income tax purposes from interest earned in the first year of winding up the estate.

After the visit to the probate registry, if inheritance tax is payable on the estate and arrangements have not been made to pay it out of National Savings or from certificates of tax deposits, the Capital Taxes Office (or Capital Taxes Business Stream as it has recently been renamed) will write to the applicants with a note of the amount of the tax it provisionally assesses to be due and with instructions as to how to make payment.

After any inheritance tax and the Probate Registry's fees have been paid, the Probate Registry will send the grant of representation to the applicant by post. This does not necessarily mean that the Capital Taxes Business Stream has finally agreed the figures entered on the forms and on the basis of which the tax is calculated are correct. The Capital Taxes Business Stream might write with further questions and demanding further tax and because the personal representative is primarily responsible for payment of tax, it is wise to write to the office asking for a formal clearance certificate from inheritance tax before finally passing the estate's money to those entitled. Formal clearance is obtained by sending to Capital Taxes Business Stream a Form IHT 30 in duplicate, one copy of which the Revenue will return signed on behalf of the Revenue if it is satisfied that all the tax which is payable has been paid. The form can be obtained by post or downloaded from the Capital Taxes Business Stream's website.

## REGISTERING THE GRANT
### What registration involves – in general

Registering the grant means producing it to the organisations, e.g. banks, with which the deceased had assets as proof of the personal representative's right to deal with the relevant asset.

At the interview with the Probate Registry the applicants will have been asked how many official copies (called office copies) of the grant were required and the copies will have been sent to the applicants with the original grant. An office copy bears the impression of the registry's seal and is as good evidence of the right to deal with the assets of the estate as is the original grant. When dealing with the title to land it is sometimes necessary to endorse a record of the dealing on the original grant of representation and produce it later to show that the endorsement was made. Moreover an original grant of representation by virtue of its nature cannot be replaced. For these reasons when registering representation, and for fear of the original grant being lost in transit, it is usual to register an office copy of the grant rather than the original grant.

Sometimes it is necessary to send passbooks or share certificates when sending an office copy grant for registration and it is suggested that reference be made to the specimen letters which are to be found in Appendix 1. Quoting the passbook or share certificate account numbers in the letters and keeping a copy of the letters will possibly assist should the original documents be lost in transit.

### Shares, debentures and loan stock

An official copy of the grant should be sent to the company's registrars with the relevant certificates as soon as possible so that the registrars will be aware that future interest and dividend cheques should be made payable to the personal representatives and not to the deceased and to facilitate any subsequent sale or transfer of the shares or stock.

If it is intended to transfer the shares or loan stock to one or more beneficiaries, a completed transfer deed should be sent to the company's registrars with the relevant share or loan stock certificate and office copy of the grant. Transfer deeds can be obtained from law stationers or from the company's registrars and are simplicity itself to complete, but it should be noted that there is a section to be completed on the back of the deed.

The address of the relevant company's registrars can be obtained from the tax voucher which is sent with dividend or interest payments, from the company's website on the Internet or from the company's annual report. The address is also usually printed on share certificates, but one should be aware that companies do change their registrars from time to time and the registrar named on the share certificate might not be the current one, especially if the security has been held for some time.

### Dividend or interest cheques

If dividend or interest cheques payable to the deceased have been received since the death took place, it will be necessary to send an office copy of the grant to the drawer of the cheque with a request that a replacement cheque be issued or the old cheque be amended into the name of the personal representative and the amendment initialled by the drawer.

### Insurance monies and pension arrears
The companies involved will have been written to when they were notified of the death and asked to state their requirements to enable payment to be made and these should now be complied with.

If the policy cannot be found the company will pay out upon an indemnity being given and a statutory declaration being made as to the circumstances. Usually the companies will prepare and supply these documents.

### Debts owed to the estate
If the deceased was owed money when he died or money became due to him as a result of the death or payable to him since death, an office copy of the grant should be sent to the debtor with a request that payment be made to the executors.

### Property which is security for a mortgage or any other liability
Instructions should not be given for the transfer, sale or other realisation of any such property unless the personal representative is absolutely certain that the estate is solvent, i.e. that there will be sufficient assets to cover payment of inheritance tax, the funeral and other expenses, debts and liabilities, because if this is not the case the creditor has a right to take and sell the property and

prove in bankruptcy for any balance of his claim. If the sale produces more than is owed the creditor must account to the estate for the amount by which the net proceeds of the sale exceed the debt.

(9)

# Paying Off the Debts and Discharging the Liabilities of the Estate

Remember before distributing the estate that the final position in respect of taxes (including tax on income received since death and prior to final distribution of the estate) must be established by completing income tax returns for the administration period and any outstanding tax paid.

## ADVERTISEMENTS FOR CREDITORS AND CLAIMANTS

Before distributing the assets of the estate among the beneficiaries, a personal representative who has not already done so should consider publishing the statutory advertisement for claimants and creditors referred to under 'Debts and liabilities' on p. 70 for the reason given there.

## WHAT DEBTS AND LIABILITIES MUST BE PAID?

Most debts, contracts and liabilities of a person survive death and must be paid or fulfilled by the personal representative. An exception is that contracts to the performance of which the personality of the deceased is essential, e.g. of a musician to perform at a concert or an author to write a book, do not survive death. The personal representative has a right to be reimbursed, out of the assets of the estate, for the payments he makes and the liabilities he incurs in the performance of his duties. He has no right to claim payment for work done in respect of the estate unless the will authorises payment.

## TO WHOM SHOULD PAYMENT BE MADE?
### Bankrupts

Payment should not be made to a beneficiary or to a creditor who is bankrupt; the entitlement is that of the trustee in bankruptcy. To discover whether a person is or is not bankrupt a search should be made against that person's name in the Alphabetical Index of Names at the Land Charges Registry. The current fee for such a search is £1 per name and search forms can be purchased from law stationers. In the event of difficulty a solicitor can be requested to make the search.

### Persons of unsound mind

Similarly, if a debt is owing to a person who is not believed to be of sound mind, the debt should not be paid to that person personally but to his receiver or to his attorney appointed under an enduring power of attorney executed before the creditor lost his sanity.

### Future debts

If the personal representative knows of debts or liabilities of the estate which might arise in the future, then before distributing the estate, he should protect himself and make provision for settling them. He can do this by:

1. obtaining an indemnity from the beneficiary against such claims; or

2. retaining a sufficient sum from the property in respect of which the liability may arise or if the liability is not contingent in respect of any particular asset of the estate, from the general estate; or

3. asking a court to direct him as to what should be done to cover the liability.

The risk with course 1 is that an indemnity is only as good financially as the person who gives it, the problem with course 2 is quantifying the extent of the liability and obtaining the beneficiary's agreement to that sum, and the problem with course 3 is the expense to the estate of the court application.

## INSOLVENT ESTATES

In cases in which the assets of the estate are sufficient to pay all the funeral and testamentary expenses and the debts and liabilities of the deceased, there is no problem as to which should be paid, but if the estate is insolvent, i.e. the assets are insufficient to pay them all, there is a complicated special order in which they must be discharged. It is as well to consult a solicitor if the estate is insolvent because a personal representative who wrongly pays a creditor before another who has precedence incurs personal liability to the wronged creditor.

# Distributing the Remaining Assets

## FINALISING AND OBTAINING CLEARANCE FROM INHERITANCE TAX

If inheritance tax has been paid on stock exchange securities (other than those quoted on the Alternative Investment Market (AIM)), shares in common investment funds, unit trusts, and land or buildings which are sold in the course of administration of the estate at a loss compared with their value as declared in the probate papers, it might be worth reconsidering the value attributed to them for inheritance tax purposes with a view to obtaining a partial refund of the tax.

In the case of stock exchange securities, shares in common investment funds and unit trusts, the personal representatives must have sold them within 12 months of the date of the death. To recalculate the amount of tax properly payable, the loss is deducted from the declared value of the estate and is calculated by deducting the *gross* proceeds of sale from the value declared for probate purposes. No allowance is made for the expenses of sale and all the quoted investments in the estate must be taken into account, not merely those sold at a loss. If the personal representatives reinvest the proceeds of sale by buying further unit trusts, common investment funds or quoted investments within two months of the last sale during the 12-month period, the amount of repayable tax will be restricted.

Similar principles apply in the case of land or buildings, the differences being that the period for the sale is four years instead of 12 months, the period for reinvestment is four months after the last qualifying sale in the period of three years from death instead of two months during the period of 12 months from death, and sales at a profit in the fourth year after death or which result in a profit or loss of less than 5 per cent or £1,000 are ignored.

It is wise to write to the Capital Taxes Office and request a formal inheritance tax clearance certificate, i.e. formal confirmation that no claim will be made by the Revenue for further inheritance tax, before distributing any assets to beneficiaries. A clearance certificate will protect the personal representative against future claims for inheritance tax in relation to the estate and give him the confidence of knowing that all the valuations have been accepted by the Revenue for inheritance tax purposes.

## THE POSSIBILITY OF CLAIMS UNDER THE INHERITANCE (PROVISION FOR FAMILY AND DEPENDANTS) ACT 1975 AS AMENDED

The personal representative should also wait for six months from the date of the grant of representation being issued by the registry before distributing any assets to beneficiaries because of the possibility of claims being made against the estate under the Inheritance (Provision for Family and Dependants) Act 1975 as amended. It is not proposed to deal with this Act in detail because if a claim is made immediate assistance should be sought from a solicitor. In broad terms the act permits anyone who considers that he was dependant on the deceased to a material extent during the deceased's lifetime to claim a share of the estate after the death, even if the will leaves the claimant nothing. A different sex partner who has been cohabiting with the deceased for two years immediately prior to death can claim without having to prove dependence. Claims have to be made within six months or, in exceptional circumstances, such other longer period as a court in its discretion, exercised in accordance with legally defined principles, permits.

## VARYING THE TERMS OF A WILL OR THE RULES OF INTESTACY AFTER DEATH

It is common knowledge that one can vary the provisions of a will during one's lifetime, but it is not so well known that the provisions of a valid will or the normal laws of inheritance applicable on intestacy are sometimes, quite legally, changed after one's death.

### Types of variation
The changes may take place either:

◆ with the consent of all the beneficiaries affected (usually set out in a deed known as a deed of family arrangement); or

- with the consent of one or more beneficiaries (as when a surviving spouse decides to exercise the right given to her by the law in the case of an intestacy to take a capital sum in lieu of income for life or a beneficiary under a will disclaims the inheritance); or

- without the consent of the beneficiaries as a result of, say, a successful claim under the Inheritance (Provision for Family and Dependants) Act 1975 as amended.

**Reasons to vary**

The reasons for wishing to change the terms of a will are many and various, for example:

- Sometimes a will has not been updated for many years and the circumstances in which it was made may have completely changed by the date of death.

- Sometimes it is decided to settle claims made under the Inheritance (Provision for Family and Dependants) Act 1975 as amended by entering into an out-of-court settlement.

- Instead of settling the question by an expensive application to a court, executors and beneficiaries might wish to settle problems created by poor drafting or typing of the will by agreement and to record the agreement in writing rather than risk further disputes.

- It might be desired to give executors wider powers than are provided for in the will, e.g. to widen the executors' powers in relation to the investment of bequests made to underage beneficiaries.

- The beneficiaries might wish to provide for someone considered to have been overlooked or wealthy persons might wish to substitute bequests to their children or grandchildren for bequests to themselves.

- The most common reason of all is to alter the provisions of the will in such a way as to ensure that less tax is incurred, although alterations purely for the purpose of saving tax are open to challenge by the Inland Revenue.

### The difference between a variation and a disclaimer

Some changes to the provisions of a will or to the devolution of an estate under the laws of intestacy can save very considerable amounts of tax if the estate is large, but others increase the amount of tax payable. The changes can affect not only inheritance tax, but also capital gains tax, income tax and means tested Social Security benefit payments, and may cost substantial sums in Stamp Duty and legal fees to implement, but in the right circumstances and if carefully and knowledgeably done, they can be very worthwhile. It is essential that advice should be taken from a solicitor or accountant who is knowledgeable about tax law before such a course of action is finally embarked upon. Suffice it to say here that if a change is to be made, the difference between disclaiming something to be inherited from a will or under the laws of intestacy and varying the provisions of a will or the laws of intestacy must be clearly understood.

To disclaim a benefit under a will or an entitlement under an intestacy is to refuse to accept it and although a disclaimer can be retracted, it can only be retracted if no other person has relied upon it to their detriment and if the person seeking to disclaim has not already benefited from the inheritance which it is sought to disclaim. The inherited benefit cannot be accepted as to part and refused as to part; it is all or nothing, although if more than one gift is made to the same beneficiary in a will or inherited on intestacy, one gift may be accepted and the other or others may be refused and disclaimed, provided they are clearly separate gifts.

On the other hand, to effect a variation one first accepts the gift and then varies it so that another or others benefit, either in addition to or to the exclusion of oneself. This point is very important because it necessarily follows that having accepted the inheritance in the case of a variation, one can decide its further devolution and decide who is to benefit from it, but having refused the inheritance in the case of a disclaimer one has no further control over it and it must devolve according to the other provisions of the will or the laws of intestacy, as the case may be.

It necessarily follows that different inheritance, capital gains and income tax consequences result from the difference in the nature of a disclaimer and a variation, and as stated above, before making a decision, it is essential that specialist tax advice be sought.

### Conditions for tax-effective variations and disclaimers
If the Revenue is to consider the change as having been made by the deceased and there is to be a saving of

inheritance and/or capital gains tax, the following conditions must be complied with.

♦ The change must be made in writing and in the case of a variation all the parties affected must be parties to the document to show they consent to the changes. However, in the case of a disclaimer, only the person making the disclaimer is a party to the document.

♦ The disclaimer or variation must be made within two years of the death.

♦ In the case of a variation, written notice must be given to the Inland Revenue by those affected and within six months of the date of the document which makes the variation, unless the variation was made after 31 July 2002 and the document effecting the variation states that it is to have effect for the purposes of inheritance tax and/or capital gains tax.

To consent to the change a party must be of full age and have full legal capacity. If this is a problem, for example if a person is under the age of 18, or not of sound mind or if a benefit which it is desired to change has been given to a person who has not yet been born, a court can be asked to consent on that person's behalf, but a court will only give consent if it considers that the transaction is for that person's benefit. Moreover, an application to a court is expensive. The fact that court proceedings are not quick can also make it difficult to comply with the six-month and two-year deadlines which will not usually be extended.

Suffice it to say here that these matters are not for a layman, and if it is thought that circumstances exist in which they might be of assistance, prompt professional assistance should be sought.

## INTEREST ON LEGACIES

Interest is payable on pecuniary, i.e. money, legacies from the date from which they are properly payable and in the absence of any provision in the will that is one year from the date of death. Legacies can be paid earlier than one year from the date of death, if convenient, but should not be paid less than six months from the date of the issue of the grant of representation in case a successful claim is made under the Inheritance (Provision for Family and Dependants) Act 1975 as amended.

## INTERPRETING A WILL AND DECIDING WHAT BEQUESTS AND LIABILITIES SHOULD BE FULFILLED

The first thing to do when considering a will is to make sure that it is the last legally effective will. Remember that going through a marriage ceremony after the date of a will itself revokes the will unless the will expressly states that it is made with that particular marriage in mind and is to continue in force after the marriage.

### Bequests which fail

*The effect of divorce or annulment of marriage*

Divorce does not invalidate a will, but a divorce decree absolute (not a decree nisi) makes any bequest in the will to the spouse take effect as if the former spouse had died on the date the decree becomes absolute, leaving bequests in the remainder of the will valid. Usually the bequest will become part of the residue of the estate and go to the residuary beneficiaries, but if the bequest is of the entire estate or of a share of the residue of the estate, it will be treated as not having been disposed of by the will and will be inherited according to the laws of intestacy.

Similarly, the provisions in a will conferring powers of appointment on a spouse (i.e. power for a spouse to appoint or choose a beneficiary for part of an estate) or appointing a spouse as an executor or trustee take effect after a decree of divorce or annulment of marriage as if the former spouse had died on the date the decree became absolute.

Unless a contrary intention is apparent from the will, an appointment of a spouse as a guardian of an underage child is revoked by a decree of divorce or annulment which is either made in a court in England or Wales or would be recognised by such a court.

*Bequests to the witness to a will or witness's spouse*
Although a person who is named in a will as the beneficiary will lose the bequest if the beneficiary or the beneficiary's spouse witnessed the will, the remainder of the will will not be affected.

*Inalienable gifts and bequests contrary to public policy*
Gifts may be void and of no effect because they are contrary to the public policy of the moment or because they tie up the subject of the gift for an excessively long time. If in doubt, take legal advice.

*Irreconcilable bequests*

Generally speaking, if two clauses of a will are clearly irreconcilable, effect should be given to the later bequest and not to the former, but again, if there is the slightest doubt, take legal advice.

*Insufficient assets*

If there are insufficient assets to pay all the debts and liabilities there is a specific complicated order in which the debts must be paid and it is wise to seek legal advice.

Properly payable debts, liabilities of the estate and funeral and testamentary expenses are payable in priority to bequests made by the will or claims to entitlement by the next of kin.

When there is sufficient money to pay all the funeral and testamentary expenses and the debts and liabilities of the deceased, but insufficient to pay all the beneficiaries named in the will, then unless there is any contrary provision in the will, those who are bequeathed specific things should have their bequests first, followed by those who are bequeathed specific amounts of money. If there is not enough to pay all the gifts of money they are reduced in proportion.

*Bequests to people who have predeceased the testator or*
*organisations which have ceased to exist*

Unless there is a provision to the contrary in the will or the gift is made to fulfil a moral or legal obligation (e.g. to repay a debt which has been discharged under the law of bankruptcy or which is statute barred), a gift made by will to a person who predeceased the testator or to an organisation which no longer exists at the time of the testator's death fails and does not take effect.

*Bequests of items which no longer exist*
If the testator no longer has such an article as is described in a gift (e.g. my gold watch where the watch has been sold or lost after the making of the will), the gift does not take effect, but if the testator, having had such an article, disposes of it and acquires another fitting the description (i.e. another gold watch), the gift takes effect in respect of the substituted object (the new gold watch). In other words, unless there is evidence that the contrary is intended as regards things given by will, the will takes effect in the circumstances which exist at the moment of death. However, this rule does not apply to the description of persons in whose favour gifts are made by will, e.g. a gift to 'John's wife', the rule being that the bequest is to the person who fulfilled the description at the time that the will was made and only if there is no such person does the person who fulfils the description at the time of death or later inherit.

*Gifts of other people's property*
There is a rule in English law known as the doctrine of election to the effect that a person who accepts a benefit conferred by a document must also accept every other provision of that document and give up any other right he possesses which is inconsistent with the document. Thus if a testator who does not own an asset purports to give it away by his will and also gives a gift to the true

owner of the asset, the true owner must either refuse his bequest or give up his own property or the value in compensation to the other beneficiary.

Perhaps an example will make the point clearer. If Farmer George dies and leaves 'my farm Blackacre to my son William and my London flat to my brother Jack' but in fact he does not own Blackacre which belongs to Jack, Jack must decide whether he will take the flat and give up Blackacre or its value to William or decline the bequest of the flat.

### Legacies to creditors

Unless an intention to the contrary is shown, there is a presumption that a legacy to a creditor which is equal to or greater than the debt owed is given in satisfaction and payment of the debt. An intention may be shown to the contrary if, for example, the will directs the executor to pay all the testator's debts or if the legacy is payable only at a future date or upon the happening of an event in the future.

### Substitutional legacies

In the absence of evidence to the contrary, if a will bequeaths the same thing or an identical sum, twice, to the same legatee, the legatee is only entitled to one of the legacies and it is presumed that the second legacy is a repetition of the first. If the two legacies are of unequal amounts or are given in different documents, e.g. one in a will and the other in a codicil to the will, the presumption does not apply and both are payable.

*Meaning of 'children'*
The word 'children' in a will or codicil means children and does not include grandchildren, unless the will shows a contrary intention or unless the context or circumstances so require.

The law in relation to wills and devolution of estates on an intestacy makes no distinction between adopted, legitimate and illegitimate children and a reference to children is taken to include them all, unless there is an indication to the contrary.

## DISTRIBUTION IN ACCORDANCE WITH THE LAWS OF INTESTACY

If someone dies without making a will he is said to die intestate and his estate is inherited according to intestacy law. A few general points first.

Intestacy law divides relatives into groups or classes according to their blood relationship to the deceased, e.g. children, siblings, grandparents, etc. All members of a given class inherit in equal shares. If a member of one class has died before the deceased and leaves issue who survive the deceased, the issue inherit the share which their predeceasing parent would have inherited had he survived, equally between them. There is a specific order in which the various classes inherit and if all members of a given class have died before the deceased without leaving issue who survived the deceased, the next class inherits. The words 'child' and 'children' are used to mean a person's immediate descendants (as opposed to grandchildren) and do not include a stepchild or stepchildren. The word 'issue' is used to include children and/or grandchildren. If those entitled to inherit are under the age of 18, the inheritance is held in trust for them until they either reach the age of 18 or marry under that age. Net estate means the estate after deducting all debts, liabilities, inheritance tax and funeral and testamentary expenses.

To decide who is entitled to inherit, look for the first class and if there is no member of the class who survived the deceased or predeceased him without leaving issue who survived him, move on to the next class.

The first person to have a claim on the estate is the surviving spouse and the amount to which the spouse is entitled depends upon the size of the estate and whether or not there are any surviving issue or certain other close relatives. If the spouse survived, but for a period of less than 28 days beginning on the day on which the intestate died, the spouse is considered to have not survived the intestate.

*If the deceased left a surviving spouse but no issue and no parent, brother or sister of the whole blood or issue of a brother or sister of the whole blood,* the surviving spouse inherits the entire estate.

*If the deceased left a surviving spouse and issue or any of the specified relatives,* the surviving spouse is entitled to the deceased's personal chattels, i.e. moveable items such as sporting trophies or motor car, but personal chattels does not include items used in any business, e.g. a delivery van.

The surviving spouse is also entitled to a fixed sum of money known as a statutory legacy and interest on the statutory legacy until payment at the rate of 6 per cent from the date of death.

If the deceased is survived by issue the spouse's statutory legacy is £125,000. If there is no surviving issue but there is a surviving parent, brother or sister of the whole blood surviving or issue of a brother or sister of the whole blood who died before the deceased, the legacy is £200,000.

The surviving spouse is further entitled to one half of what is known as 'the residuary estate', i.e. what remains of the net estate after deducting the personal chattels and the statutory legacy. If there are surviving issue, the surviving spouse is entitled to the share of the residuary estate only during the lifetime of the surviving spouse, but if there is no surviving issue, then the surviving spouse is entitled to the share for the spouse's use and benefit absolutely. Where the spouse is only entitled to the half share of the residuary estate during the spouse's remaining lifetime, because it has to be left for those who are entitled to inherit it after the spouse's own death, the spouse can only spend the income that share produces and cannot spend the capital sum represented by the share. Where the spouse is entitled to the share for his own use and benefit absolutely the spouse can, of course, dispose of both the capital and income as he wishes.

The surviving spouse is entitled to require the personal representative to use the residuary estate to purchase his interest for life in the one half share of the residuary estate from him. If the matrimonial home is freehold or leasehold with at least two years of the lease unexpired at the date of death, the spouse can also insist, within a year of the issue of the grant of representation, upon using his share of the residuary estate to buy the matrimonial home, paying any difference in value in cash. In cases where the matrimonial home:

- is part of a building or agricultural estate contained in the residuary estate or

- used in part or entirely as a hotel or lodging house or

- in part for other than domestic purposes

the right cannot be exercised unless a court is satisfied that it is not likely to diminish the value of the other assets in the residuary estate or make them more difficult to dispose of.

- *If the deceased left a surviving spouse* and issue, the issue inherit one half of the residuary estate on the deceased's death and the other one half of the residuary estate after the death of the surviving spouse.

- *If the deceased left a surviving spouse and no issue*, the one half share of the residuary estate not inherited by the surviving spouse absolutely is inherited by the deceased's parent if one survives him, or if no parent has survived, by brothers or sisters of the whole blood and issue of deceased brothers and sisters of the whole blood, the issue of the deceased brothers or sisters inheriting equally between them the share which their deceased parent would have taken had he survived.

◆ *If the deceased left no surviving spouse but left issue*, the net estate is held for the issue.

◆ *If the deceased left no surviving spouse and left no issue but left a parent or parents*, the net estate is held for the parent, and if both, then for them equally.

◆ *If the deceased left no spouse, issue or parent*, the net estate is inherited by the following classes of people living at the death and in the following order so that if there is no one in a class living at the death the subsequent class inherit, namely brothers and sisters of the whole blood, or if none, brothers and sisters of the half blood, or if none, grandparents, or if none, uncles and aunts of the whole blood, or if none, uncles and aunts of the half blood.

◆ *If the deceased was survived by none of the above*, the estate goes to the Crown or the Duchy of Cornwall or the Duchy of Lancaster.

A person is considered to be a spouse for the purposes of the laws of intestacy until a decree absolute (not a decree nisi) of divorce or a judicial separation (other than in the magistrates' court) has been pronounced.

## TO WHOM SHOULD DISTRIBUTIONS BE MADE?
### Bankrupts
Payment should not be made to a beneficiary who is bankrupt and the same points as are noted above on p. 80 in relation to payment of debts to bankrupts apply to payments of entitlements to bankrupt beneficiaries.

### Persons of unsound mind

Similarly, if a bequest has been made to a person who is not believed to be of sound mind, the bequest should not be paid to that person personally but to his receiver or to his attorney appointed under an enduring power of attorney executed before the beneficiary lost his sanity.

### Beneficiaries who cannot be found

Sometimes a beneficiary may have disappeared and cannot be traced even after advertisement for them. In such a case the deceased's will should be checked to see if it contains directions as to whether the contingency is provided for and if not a solicitor should be instructed to pay the bequest into court or to make an application to a court for directions as to what should be done.

### Underage beneficiaries

Unless permitted to do so by the will, neither a person under the age of 18 nor that person's parent or guardian can give a valid receipt for capital, as opposed to income and consequently cannot give a valid discharge for any capital payment made to him. Accordingly a personal representative should not make any such payment unless authorised by the will and should either retain the sum due in the personal representative's name on behalf of the underage beneficiary until the beneficiary becomes of age or arrange for it to be paid into court.

If the bequest is retained in the personal representative's name, it should be invested in authorised investments and be designated as in respect of the beneficiary to avoid the possibility of the investments being confused with the personal investments of the personal representative.

Authorised investments are those authorised by the will or other document creating the trust and in addition those permitted by Part II (sections 3–7) of the Trustee Act 2000. The Act gives trustees and personal representatives (who will for the purpose of conciseness both be referred to in this section as 'the trustee') the same powers to invest money as they would have if they owned the monies themselves, but also provides that:

- any restrictions or other provisions contained in the will or other document creating the trust, if dated after 3 of August 1961, must be complied with;

- the trustee has a duty to use such skill and care in the choice of investments and advisers as is reasonable bearing in mind any special knowledge, experience and professional skill of the trustee and the nature and purpose of the trust;

- in the choice of investments a trustee must bear in mind the need for diversification, i.e. he must not put all the eggs in one basket;

- the investments should be kept under review with a view to deciding whether or not they should be varied; and

- unless it is not appropriate that they should do so or unnecessary, trustees should obtain and consider proper advice as to how the power of investment should be exercised and the suitability of the investments to the trust. It might not be appropriate to take advice if, for example, the trustee himself has the necessary investment skills and knowledge or if the cost of the advice would be out of proportion to the value of the investments.

## TRANSFERRING BUILDINGS OR LAND
Leasehold property is special in that the lease under which the property is held sometimes contains provisions requiring the death certificate, probate or letters of administration to be registered, i.e. produced to, the landlord within specified time limits so that the landlord is kept aware of the identity of his tenant and a fee is to be paid to the landlord for his trouble. In theory failure to register the document with the landlord could result in loss of the lease so the matter should not be overlooked.

When transferring leasehold property care must also be taken to check whether or not there are any outstanding liabilities such as arrears of ground rent or dilapidations under the lease and reference should be made to the will to determine who is to bear them. A personal representative transferring leasehold property to a beneficiary would be wise to ensure that the transfer deed contains a provision by the beneficiary which indemnifies the personal representative against existing and future dilapidations in respect of the property.

Freehold properties and leasehold properties have either an unregistered or a registered title. A registered one is one which has been investigated by the Land Registry and one in respect of which the Land Registry has issued a title document called a Land Certificate (or if the property is mortgaged, a Charge Certificate), certifying the quality and details of the title. If there is no such document with the title documents it is virtually certain that the title is not a registered one, but the position should be checked by submitting a search of the Public Index Map to the relevant District Land Registry. Such a search is free unless more than ten titles are involved in which case the current fee is £4 for each additional title. The search can be done by post on Land Registry Form number 096. Land Registry forms can be obtained from the District Land Registry, from a law stationer, or downloaded for private use from the Land Registry's website at www.landreg.gov.uk on the Internet.

The name of the relevant District Land Registry appears in the Land Certificate or in the Charge Certificate and can also be obtained from the Land Registry website at www.landreg.gov.uk.

If the title is not a registered one, it is now necessary to ask the Land Registry to register it, unless the property is leasehold and the lease has less than 21 years to run. Preparation of an application to register a title can only be safely done by someone with a considerable knowledge of property law and is best done by a solicitor.

If the title has previously been registered in joint names, on the death of one of the registered owners, it is necessary to send a registrar's copy of the death certificate and a completed Land Registry form 083 to the District Land Registry where the title is registered so that the death can be noted on the registers of the title. In any other case, unless before the death the property was owned by one or more people as joint tenants, it will be necessary to prepare a transfer of it to the beneficiary entitled on the death and to register the transfer with The Land Registry when finally winding up the estate. In either case the Land or Charge certificate, as the case may be and Land Registry form AP1 should accompany the other documents to the Land Registry so that it can be amended to note the change of ownership.

If the property was owned by one person before his death and is to be transferred to one other person after the death, the transfer is done on a Land Registry form number AS1 or AS3. Form AS1 is used if all the property covered by the Land Certificate or Charge Certificate is to be transferred and form AS3 if only part of the property is to be transferred. The forms are easy to complete and after completion should be sent to the relevant District Land Registry with an office copy of the grant of representation, a completed Land Registry Form of Application to Register a Dealing (form number AP1), the Land or Charge Certificate and the appropriate Land Registry fee.

The amount of the relevant fees payable to the Land Registry and the Land Registry forms can be obtained from the Registry or downloaded for personal use from the Land Registry website at www.landreg.gov.uk.

In any other case ask a solicitor or licensed conveyancer to prepare the transfer and effect the registration.

## TRANSFERRING SHARES OR STOCK

The steps to be taken are described on p. 76.

## FINAL ACCOUNTS

Finally, before distributing the estate to the beneficiaries, the personal representative would be well advised to get accounts approved by the residuary beneficiaries and to get a form of receipt and discharge from all the beneficiaries. If they will not sign an application for a formal discharge can be made to a court.

It should be noted here that an executor is not entitled to charge for the work he has done or the time he has expended in connection with the estate unless the will provides to the contrary, but he is entitled to be reimbursed for out-of-pocket expenses he has incurred.

A suitable form of account and receipt for the estate outlined on pp. 52–53 might be as follows:

---

### ESTATE ACCOUNTS RELATING TO THE ESTATE OF THE LATE A.A.B.

A.A.B. died on 30 January 2003 having appointed his sons A.B. and C.B. to be the executors of his last will dated 22 June 2002. By the will A.A.B. devised his house 23 Church Street Hove Sussex to his son A.B. and after leaving legacies of £10,000.00 to each of his friends E.F. and I.J., A.A.B. gave the remainder of his estate to his son C.B. and his daughter K.L. in equal shares. I.J. predeceased the testator on

---

2 November 2002. The executors proved the will in the Brighton District Probate Registry on 22 March 2003.

## CASH ACCOUNT

| | £ |
|---|---:|
| 23 Church Street Hove Sussex transferred to A.B. | 180,000.00 |
| Furniture and effects | 15,000.00 |
| Of Big Insurance Co. – proceeds of life policy | 10,000.00 |
| Of Barclays Bank Plc. – balance on current account | 300.00 |
| Of Nationwide Building Society – balance on account | 1290.10 |
| Of Yorkshire Building Society – balance on account | 6709.90 |
| Of Nationwide Building Society – balance on ISA account | 12,000.00 |
| By encashment of Premium Savings Bonds | 700.00 |
| By encashment of Pensioners Bonds | 2,000.00 |
| Cash in house | 100.00 |
| Shares in Abbey National Plc | 1,020.50 |
| Shares in Northern Rock Plc | 2,205.00 |
| Shares in Severn Trent Water | 1,005.50 |
| Shares in British Energy Plc | 1,669.00 |
| Interest between death and closure on building society accounts | 60.50 |
| Interest between death and closure on Pensioners Bonds | 20.00 |
| Dividend received since death | 15.50 |

| | | £ |
|---|---|---|
| Gain on shares sold during the administration of the estate | | 80.20 |
| Total | | 234,176.20 |

| Deduct | £ | |
|---|---|---|
| Income tax | 4.00 | |
| Funeral account and post-funeral meal | 1,400.00 | |
| Probate fees | 400.00 | |
| Cost of statutory advertisement for creditors | 117.50 | |
| HM Land Registry fee on transfer of house | 50.00 | |
| Executor's expenses and cost of death certificates | 76.00 | 2,047.50 |

| | | |
|---|---|---|
| Balance carried to Distribution Account | | 232,128.70 |

## DISTRIBUTION ACCOUNT

| | £ | £ |
|---|---|---|
| Balance from Cash Account | | 232,128.70 |
| Less: | | |
| To A.B. bequest of 23 Church Street Hove | 180,000.00 | |
| To E.F. legacy | 10,000.00 | |
| To C.B. ½ share of residue | 21,064.35 | |
| To K.L. ½ share of residue | 21,064.35 | 232,128.70 |

We A.B., E.F., C.B. and K.L. approve and agree the above accounts and acknowledge that we have received from A.B. and C.B., the executors of the estate, the above bequests in full satisfaction of all claims by us against the estate and the executors of the will.

Signed by A.B. this          day of          2003

_____

Signed by E.F. this          day of          2003

_____

Signed by C.B. this          day of          2003

_____

Signed by K.L. this          day of          2003

_____

Before submitting the accounts for the approval of the beneficiaries care should be taken to reconcile the accounts with the bank statements by ensuring that the balance of the Cash Account, after making allowances for anything transferred to beneficiaries without being turned into cash, agrees with the final sum withdrawn from the bank account. If it does not there must be an error in the bank statement or, more likely, an omission from or other error in the accounts.

## TAX AND INCOME EARNED DURING THE ADMINISTRATION PERIOD

If the estate earned income from the estate assets or they rose in value between the date of death and the date they were cashed, the personal representatives and the estate must account for any chargeable income and capital gains tax. Some of the interest may have been taxed at source, i.e. before it was paid to the estate, but other income such as rent and interest on Pensioners Bonds is paid to the executors without any deduction of tax and is taxable at the standard rate in the hands of the executors to whom no personal allowances are available. The personal representatives are entitled to an annual exemption from capital gains tax equivalent to that of an individual in the year of death and the following two years. The beneficiaries are entitled to credit for tax paid on their share of the income of the estate which was earned between death and distribution of the estate and they must show the tax and income in their own tax returns. To enable the beneficiaries to deal with the tax on income, the executors must complete for each beneficiary affected a short form number R185E which is obtainable from the local Income Tax Office and which will show the beneficiary's share of the tax and the income.

If the executors had needed to borrow to pay the inheritance tax and probate fees, the interest paid on the borrowing could have been deducted from the interest received by the estate in working out the figures to complete form R185E.

Form R185 and the above remarks in relation to it apply equally to administrators and intestacies.

# Appendix 1
# Specimen Forms and Letters

## SPECIMEN FORM OF LIVING WILL

1. I (*insert your full names, address and occupation, if any*), on the (*insert the date*) make this Living Will and set down as guidance to my family and my medical practitioners these advance directions as to the types of medical treatment I would and would not wish to undergo bearing in mind that in the future I might be unable to express my wishes.

2. IN giving these directions I consider that:
   - I am in good physical health

   - I am mentally competent

   - I have considered the matter thoroughly

   - I believe myself to be fully informed and

   - I do so voluntarily and free from influence by others.

3. IF any of the conditions specified in the First Schedule below apply to me and in the opinion of (*insert number*) medical practitioners I am unlikely to recover a good quality of life THEN I would not

wish to undergo any of the treatments specified in the Second Schedule below but would wish attempts to be made to prolong my life by the treatments specified in the Third Schedule below if they are appropriate.

The First Schedule referred to above – the conditions

♦ I am brain dead.

♦ I show no signs of cerebral activity.

♦ I am suffering from permanent mental impairment.

♦ I have been in a continuous coma for (*insert the number*) months.

♦ By reason of mental illness I have been unable to recognise and respond to my family or friends and I have not been aware of my surroundings or able to differentiate between night and day for (*insert the number*) of months.

♦ I am suffering from any degenerative and incurable illness.

♦ I have suffered (*insert the number*) cardiac arrests.

♦ I am totally paralysed.

♦ I am blind, dumb and deaf.

♦ I am in a persistent vegetative state.

The Second Schedule referred to above – treatment I do not wish to have

- Attempted resuscitation.

- Artificial feeding.

- Drug therapy.

- Blood transfusions.

- Artificial ventilation.

The Third Schedule referred to above – treatment I wish to have if appropriate

- Artificial feeding.

- Attempted resuscitation.

- Drug therapy.

- Blood transfusions.

- Artificial ventilation.

- Treatment to alleviate pain notwithstanding that it might shorten my life.

SIGNED by me (*insert your full names*)
(*Sign your name here*)

In the presence of (*insert full names of the witness*)
(*Witness to sign and print full names and address here*)

*Note.* The conditions and treatments set out in the schedules are specimens only and you will need to amend, omit or add to them to suit your own wishes but any attempt to prevent basic care such as feeding by mouth or washing will be ineffective.

## WORKSHEET

<u>Personal Details</u>

Full name of deceased

Usual address at death

Address in will

Occupation

Marital status

Date of birth

Date of death

Surviving relatives – husband/wife – brother(s)/ sister(s) – parents – children
Name
Number of:
  – children
  – grandchildren

National Insurance number

Income tax district and reference

Date of will

Domicile

Full names and addresses and occupations of executors

Substantial gifts made in the last seven years?

## Progress schedule

Date of grant of probate

Date of publication of advertisement for claimants

Expiry date for claims

Date inheritance tax clearance application dispatched

Date inheritance tax clearance received

Employees?

Household insurance policies
Date notified          Effected          Cancelled

Items to be returned to owners, date returned

Interest in trusts?

### Estate assets

| Asset | Date death notified | Date grant registered | Date asset realised | Sum received |
|-------|--------------------|----------------------|--------------------|--------------|
|       |                    |                      |                    |              |

### Estate Liabilities

| Creditor | Date death notified | Date debt paid |
|----------|--------------------|----------------|
|          |                    |                |

| Legacies | | | |
|---|---|---|---|
| Legatee's name | Current address | Amount | Date paid |
|  |  |  |  |

| Estate accounts | | | |
|---|---|---|---|
| Residuary beneficiary's name | Date submitted for approval | Date approved | Date distribution made |
|  |  |  |  |

## ADVERTISEMENT FOR CREDITORS AND CLAIMANTS WHERE THERE IS A WILL – LOCAL NEWSPAPER

Advertisement pursuant to Section 27 of The Trustee Act 1925 – (*insert name*) Deceased.

NOTICE IS HEREBY GIVEN pursuant to Section 27 of The Trustee Act 1925 that any person having a claim against or interest in the estate of (*insert full names*) who died on the (*insert date*) and whose will appointed (*insert executors' names and addresses*) to be the executors there of are required to send particulars in writing of their claim to the said executors by the (*insert date to be at least two months after the date of the publication of the notice*) after which date the executors will distribute the estate among the persons entitled thereto having regard only to the claims and interests of which they have then had notice.

DATED this          day of          2003

Signed                     and

Executors

## ADVERTISEMENT FOR CREDITORS AND CLAIMANTS WHERE THERE IS NO WILL – LOCAL NEWSPAPER,

Advertisement pursuant to Section 27 of The Trustee Act 1925 – (*insert name*) Deceased.

NOTICE IS HEREBY GIVEN pursuant to Section 27 of The Trustee Act 1925 that any person having a claim against or interest in the estate of (*insert full names*) who died on the (*insert date*) are required to send particulars in writing of their claim to (*insert names and addresses of the proposed personal representatives*) the proposed administrators of the estate by the (*insert date to be at least two months after the date of the publication of the notice*) after which date the administrators will distribute the estate among the persons entitled thereto having regard only to the claims and interests of which they have then had notice.

DATED this          day of          2003

Signed          and

Proposed Administrators of the Estate.

## LETTER TO ACCOMPANY ADVERTISEMENT FOR CREDITORS AND CLAIMANTS – LOCAL NEWSPAPER

To (*insert name and address of newspaper*)

Dear Sirs

(*insert name of deceased*) Deceased
I enclose advertisement pursuant to section 27 of The Trustee Act 1925 and I shall be obliged if you will arrange for its publication, once only please, in the first possible issue of (*insert name of newspaper*). Please let me have a voucher copy of the publication and your account in due course.

Yours faithfully

## TO *THE LONDON GAZETTE* REQUESTING FORM FOR ADVERTISEMENT FOR CLAIMANTS AND CREDITORS

To the Manager
The London Gazette
PO Box 7923
London SW8 5WF

Dear Sir,

I shall be obliged if you will let me have a form for completion to enable me to have an advertisement published in *The Gazette* pursuant to section 27 of The Trustee Act 1925 and a note of the fee payable.

Yours faithfully

## TO *THE LONDON GAZETTE* ENCLOSING FORM FOR ADVERTISEMENT FOR CLAIMANTS AND CREDITORS

To the Manager
The London Gazette
PO Box 7923
London SW8 5WF

Dear Sir

Advertisement pursuant to section 27 of
The Trustee Act 1925
(*insert name of the deceased*)

Please find enclosed

1. Advertisement for claimants and creditors.

2. Office copy grant of representation for inspection and return.

3. Cheque in the sum of (*insert amount*) which I understand to be the correct fee.

Please publish the advertisement in the first possible issue of the *Gazette* and let me have a voucher copy of the advertisement for my records when it has been published.

Yours faithfully

## PRE-GRANT OF REPRESENTATION LETTERS
### To banks and building societies

The Manager
(*insert name of Society or Bank*)
(*insert address*)

Dear Sir

I am the executor of the will of your customer (*insert name of the deceased*) of (*insert address*) who died on (*insert date of death*) and I enclose a registrar's death certificate and a copy of the will for noting in your records and return.

Please let me have details of all accounts which the deceased has with your organisation, and particulars of any assets or securities held for the estate.

In respect of each account please state:

1. the balance of the account as at the date of death including accrued interest

2. the interest accrued to the account between the end of the last financial year and the date of death

3. whether the interest is gross or net and if net the amount of tax deducted and

4. whether there are any direct debits or standing orders in respect of the account and if so kindly supply me with full particulars.

I shall be obliged if you will also let me know your requirements to close the accounts and let me have any necessary forms for signature.

For reasons of security I have destroyed the deceased's (*insert bank or building society as appropriate*) card(*s*) number(*s*) (*insert numbers*).

Please cancel any standing orders in respect of the accounts and do not meet any more direct debits.

All future communications should be sent to me at my above address.

Yours faithfully

*Note.* If a passbook is available, insert the following additional paragraph after the first paragraph. 'The passbook for account number (*insert number*) is enclosed to be made up to date and returned to me please.'

## To Benefits Agency

The Benefits Agency
(*insert address*)

Dear Sirs

(insert name) deceased<br>National Insurance number (insert number)

I am the executor of the will of (*insert name of the above named deceased*) of (*insert address*) who died on (*insert date of death*) and I enclose a registrar's death certificate and a copy of the will for noting in your records and return.

Please also find enclosed the deceased's pension (*insert book or card as appropriate*).

Kindly let me know the amount of any benefit which the agency claims has been overpaid so that repayment can be made when the estate is in funds or the amount of any outstanding benefit due to the estate. Please also let me know your requirements to enable payment of any outstanding benefit to be made.

All future communications should be sent to me at my above address.

Yours faithfully

**To company registrars in respect of shares and/or stock**

The Registrar
(*insert company name and address of the registrar*)

Dear Sir

The late (*insert name*)
(*insert company name and share account number,
if known*)

I am the personal representative of (*insert deceased's name*) and I enclose a death certificate for registration in your books and return.

Please let me have (*insert number of transfer deeds required*) transfer deeds for completion to enable me to transfer the holding to the beneficiaries when the grant of representation, which will be registered with you, is to hand.

Yours faithfully

## To creditors

To (*insert name and address of creditor*)

Dear Sir

Account Number (*insert number*)

I am the executor of the will of (*insert name of the deceased*) of (*insert address*) who died on (*insert date of death*) and I enclose a registrar's death certificate for noting in your records and return.

Please let me have a final statement detailing the amount claimed and in view of the death, see that no enforcement action is taken until the estate is in funds.

All future correspondence should be sent to me at the above address.

Yours faithfully

*Note.* If the creditor is a credit or debit card company add, 'I am destroying the card number (*insert number*) to avoid it being misused'.

## To employer

To (*insert name and address of employer*)

For the attention of the Salaries Department

Dear Sirs

(*insert name*) deceased, employee number
(*insert number*)

I am the executor of the will of (*insert name of the deceased*) of (*insert address*) who died on (*insert date of death*) and was employed by the company as a (*insert job title*) in the (*insert name of department*) department. A registrar's death certificate and a copy of the will are enclosed for noting in your records and return.

Please let me know:

1. Whether there are any arrears of salary or other payments due to the estate (and if so the amounts involved) and your requirements to enable them to be claimed.

2. The gross amount of salary payable in the current tax year and the deductible amount of income tax.

3. Whether to your knowledge, your late employee was a member of any pension fund and if so the name and address of the fund and the membership number.

Yours faithfully

## To household insurance companies

To the Manager
(*insert name and address of company*)

Dear Sir

Policy number (*insert number*)

I am the executor of the will of (*insert name of the deceased*) of (*insert address*) who was the holder of the above policy and who died on (*insert date of death*). A registrar's death certificate is enclosed for noting in your records and return.

The property is currently furnished but unoccupied and as executor I wish to keep the insurance in force pending clearance of the effects and disposal of the property which will take place following the issue of a formal grant of representation to the estate. Please let me know your requirements to enable this to be done.

All future communications should be sent to me at my above address.

Yours faithfully

## To Inland Revenue concerning income and capital gains tax

To HM Inspector of Taxes
(*insert name and address of inspector*)

Tax reference (*insert if known*)

Dear Sir

I am the executor of the will of (*insert name of the deceased*) of (*insert address*) who died on (*insert date of death*) and I enclose a registrar's death certificate and a copy of the will for noting in your records and return.

Please supply me with a copy of the deceased's last tax return and the appropriate forms to enable me to make a return to the date of death and in due course a personal representative's return for the period to the finalisation of the estate.

Please also let me have details of any tax now outstanding or any repayment due to the estate and the Revenue's requirements to enable these matters to be dealt with.

All future communications should be sent to me at my above address.

Yours faithfully

## To life assurance company

To (*insert name and address of company*)

Dear Sirs

Policy number (*insert policy number*)

I am the executor of the will of your customer (*insert name of the deceased*) of (*insert address*) who died on (*insert date of death*) and I enclose a registrar's death certificate and a copy of the will for noting in your records and return. The original policy and premium book are also enclosed.

Please let me know:

1. your requirements to enable the policy monies to be paid

2. whether you know of any other policies on the deceased's life with your company and

3. the sum(s) payable in respect of each policy.

Yours faithfully

## To mortgage company

To the Manager
(*insert name and address of company*)

Dear Sir,

(*insert mortgage account reference number and
address of the property mortgaged*)
(*insert name of the deceased*)

I am the executor of the will of your above named customer late of (*insert address*) who died on (*insert date of death*) and I enclose a registrar's death certificate and a copy of the will for noting in your records and return.

Please note the death in your records and let me know the amount of the capital outstanding in respect of the mortgage as at the date of the death and the date the mortgage was effected.

Kindly also let me know the amount of interest outstanding at the date of death.

If the mortgage was supported by a life or endowment policy, please let me have details of the policy including the name and current address of the company concerned and the policy number.

The grant of representation will be registered with you when it is to hand and at that date I shall let you know whether it is desired to pay off the mortgage or whether a request will be made to continue it in the beneficiary's name. Until that date please see that no enforcement action is taken.

Yours faithfully

## To National Savings Bank

To the Director of Savings
National Savings Bank
Glasgow
G58 1SB

Dear Sir

I am the executor of the will of (*insert name of the deceased*) of (*insert address*) who was the holder of account number (*insert account number*) and who died on (*insert date of death*). The passbook is enclosed together with a registrar's death certificate and copy of the will all for noting in your records and return.

Please make the book up to date and let me know the amount of interest accrued in the current tax year to the date of death.

When replying, kindly let me have the appropriate form to close the account.

All future communications should be sent to me at my above address.

Yours faithfully

## To National Savings Certificates

The Director of Savings
Savings Certificates Division
Durham
DH99 1NS

Dear Sir

I am the executor of the will of (*insert name of the deceased*) of (*insert address*) who was the holder of the certificates described below and who died on (*insert date of death*). The holder's number is (*insert the number*). A registrar's death certificate and copy of the will are enclosed for noting in your records and return.

Please let me have a note of the value of the certificates as at the date of death and the appropriate form for me to (*insert transfer or cash as is required*) the certificates when the grant of representation is to hand.

All future communications should be sent to me at my above address.

Yours faithfully

Certificate number (*insert numbers*) dated (*insert dates*) for (*insert number of units in the particular certificate*).

**Paragraph to be inserted in pre-grant letters to organisations from which money is due if the gross value of the estate is under £5,000:**

In view of the fact that it is not anticipated that the gross value of the estate will exceed £5,000 and in order to keep expenses in proportion, it is not proposed to extract a grant of representation to the estate unless you insist.

## To pension fund when pension is already being paid

The Secretary
(*insert pension fund name and address*)

Dear Sirs

> (*insert name*) deceased Pension number (*insert number*)

I am the executor of the will of your pensioner (*insert name of the deceased*) of (*insert address*) who died on (*insert date of death*) and I enclose a registrar's death certificate and a copy of the will for noting in your records and return.

Please let me know:

1. whether there are any arrears of pension due to the estate to the date of death or any overpaid pension due to be refunded to the pension fund

2. your requirements to enable you to pay any arrears

3. the gross amount of pension payable in the current tax year, including sums due to the date of death but not yet paid

4. the amount of tax deducted or which will be deducted from the current tax year's pension and

5. the address and reference number for the relevant tax district.

All future communications should be sent to me at my above address.

Yours faithfully

**To pension fund when pension is not yet being paid**

The Secretary
(*insert pension fund name and address*)

Dear Sirs

(*insert name*) deceased Pension number (*insert number if known*)

I am the executor of the will of (*insert name of the deceased*) of *(insert address)* who died on (*insert date of death*).

I understand that the deceased, who was employed by (*insert employer's name*) at (*insert address at which employed*), was a member of your scheme.

A registrar's death certificate and a copy of the will are enclosed for noting in your records and return and I shall be obliged if you will let me know what benefits are due to the deceased's estate and dependants and whether the benefits are subject to inheritance tax.

Yours faithfully

## To supply companies

To the Accounts Manager
(*insert name and address of company*)

Dear Sir

Account number (*insert number*)

I am the executor of the will of your customer (*insert name of the deceased*) of (*insert address*) who died on (*insert date of death*) and I enclose a registrar's death certificate for noting in your records and return.

Please confirm the sum claimed to the date of death and in view of the death see that no enforcement action is taken until the estate is in funds and payment can be made.

I wish to continue the supply until further notice and shall be obliged if you will let me know your requirements to enable this to be done.

All future correspondence should be sent to me at the above address.

Yours faithfully

## To trustees of a trust of which the deceased was a life tenant or annuitant

(*insert name and address of the trustees*)

Dear Sir

(*insert the name of the trust*)

I am the executor of the will of (*insert name of the deceased*) of (*insert address*) who died on (*insert date of death*) and I enclose a Registrar's death certificate and a copy of the will for noting in your records and return.

My information is that the deceased was a beneficiary of the trust and I shall be obliged if you will let me have a copy of the trust instrument and particulars of the trust fund for my information.

Please let me know the gross and net income due to the estate to the date of death.

Yours faithfully

## POST-GRANT OF REPRESENTATION
### To registrars in respect of shares and/or stock

The Registrar
(*insert company name and address*)

Dear Sir

> The late (*insert name and account number of holding if known*)

I am the personal representative of (*insert deceased's name*) and I enclose an office copy of the grant of representation for registration and return and the relevant certificates together with the uncashed (*insert dividend or interest as appropriate*) warrant (s) in respect of the holdings set out below.

Please amend or reissue the warrants in my name so that they can be paid into the estate's bank account (*insert 'and let me have new certificates in accordance with the enclosed transfer deeds' or insert 'and endorse the certificates so that I can arrange to sell the holdings' as required*).

Yours faithfully

Enclosures:

Office copy grant of representation.

(*insert company name*) certificate number (*insert number*) in respect of (*insert number in the case of shares or amount of stock in the case of loan or debenture stock*) of (*insert description of security, e.g. 25p ordinary shares or 1st Debenture stock*).

(*Insert company name*) (*insert dividend or interest as appropriate*) warrant dated (*insert date*) for (*insert amount*).

(If the security is to be transferred add '(*insert company name*) transfer deed in respect of (*insert holding to be transferred*) in favour of (*insert name of new holder*)'.

## To creditor paying account

To (*insert name and address of company*)

Dear Sirs

The estate of the late (*insert name of the deceased*)

I send herewith a cheque in the sum of £(*insert amount*) in settlement of your enclosed account. Please return to me marked as paid at your early convenience.

Yours faithfully

## To Inspector of Taxes notifying end of administration period and enclosing final tax return

HM Inspector of Taxes
(*insert address of relevant tax office*)

Tax Reference (*insert reference*)

Dear Sir

The estate of the late (*insert name of the deceased*)

No further income is anticipated in respect of the above estate and I enclose the final tax return in respect of the estate together with the certificates of deduction of tax from the income. Please return the certificates to me when they have served your purposes.

Please also accept this letter as formal notice that the administration period in respect of the above estate-ended on (*insert the date when all the assets and liabilities of the estate were known, no further income was anticipated and the liabilities had been paid and discharged*) and let me have a final tax assessment in respect of the estate.

I shall be obliged if you will also let me have (*insert the number required, one for each beneficiary entitled to income from the estate and for each tax year of the administration period*) forms R185E.

Yours faithfully

**To Inland Revenue requesting Inheritance Tax Clearance certificate**

To Capital Taxes Business Stream
Farrers House
PO Box 38
Castle Meadow Road
Nottingham
NG2 1BB

Dear Sirs

Your Reference (*insert Capital Taxes Business Stream's reference*)
The estate of the late (*insert name of the deceased*)
Date of death (*insert date*)

I shall be obliged if you will let me have a formal Inheritance Tax Clearance certificate at your early convenience.

Yours faithfully

## To residuary beneficiaries enclosing accounts for approval

To (*insert name and address of beneficiary*)

Dear

The estate of the late (*insert name of the deceased*)

I believe that I have now completed the administration of the estate and I enclose copies of the accounts in duplicate for your approval and I have similarly sent copies of the accounts to the other parties involved for their approval.

If you approve the accounts, please sign and date the form of discharge at the bottom of one copy of the accounts and return that copy to me.

When all parties have returned the accounts to me approved I shall be in a position to let you have a remittance for the sum shown as due to you by the accounts.

If you have any queries on the accounts I shall be pleased to deal with them upon hearing from you.

Yours faithfully

## Form of receipt for legacy

The estate of the late (*insert deceased's name*)

I, (*insert name of beneficiary*) of (*insert address and if different from that stated in the will add 'formerly of' and the address stated in the will*) acknowledge that I have received from (*insert your name*) the personal representative of the late (*insert the deceased's name*) (*insert description of the bequest following the description given in the will as far as possible*).

Dated

Signed

# Appendix 2
# Useful addresses

Association of British Insurers, 51 Gresham Street, London EC2V 7HQ. Tel: 020 7600 3333. www.abi.org.uk.

Bank of England Stock Office, Southgate House, Southgate Street, Gloucester GL1 1UW. Tel: 01452 398080. www.bankofengland.co.uk/registrars.

British Bankers Association, Pinners Hall, 105–108 Old Broad Street, London EC2N 1EX. Tel: 020 7216 8800. www.bba.org.uk.

Building Society's Association, 3 Saville Row, London W1S 3PB. Tel: 020 7437 0655. www.bsa.org.uk.

Capital Taxes Business Stream, Farrers House, PO Box 38, Castle Meadow Road, Nottingham NG2 1BB. Tel: 0131 7774180. www.inlandrevenue.gov.uk/cto.

Charity Commission, Harmsworth House, 13–15 Bouverie Street, London EC4Y 8DP. Tel: 0870 333 0123. www.charity-commission.gov.uk.

Coroners Section, Home Office, Constitutional and Policy Directorate, Room 972, 50 St Anne's Gate, London SW1H 9AT. Tel: 020 7273 3560.

FACTS Health Centre, 23–25 Weston Park, Crouch End, London N8 9SY. Tel: 020 8348 9195.

Financial Services Authority, 25 The North Colonnade, Canary Warf, London E14 5HS. Tel: 0845 606 1234. www.fsa.gov.uk.

FT Information Services, London EC2A 2DC. Tel: 020 825 8000. www.ft.com.

HM Inspector of Anatomy, Department of Health, Wellington House, 133–155 Waterloo Road, London SE1 8UG. Tel: 020 7972 4342. www.doh.gov.uk/hmai.

Land Registry. Tel: 020 7917 8888. www.landreg.gov.uk.

Law stationers – Oyez Straker. See website for local retail shops. Tel: 0870 737 7370. www.oyezformslink.co.uk.

Law stationers – Shaw & Sons, Shaway House, 21 Bourne Park Road, Crayford, Kent DA1 4BZ. Tel: 01322 621100. www. shaws.co.uk.

Law stationers – Stat Plus, Stat Plus House, Prince George's Road, London SW19 2PU. Tel: 020 8646 5500. www. statplus.co.uk.

London Anatomy Office, Imperial College Faculty of Medicine, Charing Cross Hospital, Fulham Palace Road, London W6 8RF. Tel: 020 8846 1216.

London Gazette, London Gazette, PO Box 7923, London SW8 5WF. Tel: 020 7873 8308. www.london-gazette.co.uk.

London Lighthouse, 52–54 Grays Inn Road, London WC1X 8JU. Tel: 020 7792 1200 or 0845 1221200. www.londonlighthouse.org.uk.

Muslim Burial Council of Leicestershire, 394 East Park Road, Leicester LE5 5HL. Tel: 0116 273 0141. www.mbcol.org.uk.

National Savings Bank, National Savings, Cowglen, Glasgow G58 1SB. Tel: 0141 6494555. www.open.gov.uk/natsav.

National Savings Capital Bonds, National Savings Capital Bonds, Cowglen, Glasgow G58 1SB. Tel: 0645 645 000. www.nationalsavings.co.uk.

National Savings Childrens Bonus Bonds, National Savings Childrens Bonus Bonds, Cowglen, Glasgow G58 1SB. Tel: 0645 645 000. www.nationalsavings.co.uk.

National Savings Deposit Bonds, National Savings Deposit Bonds, Durham DH99 1NS. Tel: 0645 645 000. www. nationalsavings.co.uk.

National Savings First Option Bonds, National Savings First Option Bonds, Cowglen, Glasgow G58 1SB. Tel: 0645 645 000. www.nationalsavings.co.uk.

National Savings Fixed Interest Savings Certificates, National Savings Certificates and SAYE Office, Milburn House, Durham DH99 1NS. Tel: 0845 964 5000. www. nationalsavings.co.uk.

National Savings Income Bonds, Income Bonds, National Savings Bonds and Stock Office, Marton Road, Blackpool FY3 9ZT. Tel: 0845 964 5000. www.nationalsavings.co.uk.

National Savings Index Linked Savings Certificates, National Savings Certificates and SAYE Office, Milburn House,

Durham DH99 1NS. Tel: 0845 964 5000. www. nationalsavings.co.uk.

National Savings ISAs, National Savings ISAs, Durham DH99 1NS. Tel: 0845 964 5000. www.nationalsavings.co.uk.

National Savings Pensioners Bonds, Pensioners Bonds, National Savings Bonds and Stock Office, Marton Road, Blackpool FY3 9YP. Tel: 0845 964 5000. www.nationalsavings.co.uk.

National Savings Premium Savings Bonds, Premium Bonds, National Savings Bonds and Stock Office, Marton Road, Blackpool FY3 9YP. Tel: 0845 964 5000. www. nationalsavings.co.uk.

National Savings SAYE Contracts, National Savings Certificates and SAYE Office, Milburn House, Durham DH99 1NS. Tel: 0845 964 5000. www.nationalsavings.co.uk.

National Savings Tracing, National Savings Tracing Office, Freepost BJ 2092, Blackpool FY3 9XR. Tel: 0845 964 5000. www.nationalsavings.co.uk.

National Savings Yearly Plan, National Savings Certificates and SAYE Office, Milburn House, Durham DH99 1NS. Tel: 0845 964 5000. www.nationalsavings.co.uk.

Natural Death Society, 20 Heber Road, London NW2 6AA. Tel: 020 8208 2853. www.naturaldeath.org.uk.

Pensions Scheme Registry, Occupational Pensions Board, PO Box 1NN, Newcastle upon Tyne NE99 1NN. Tel: 0191 225 6394. www.opra.gov.uk/registry.

Peterborough District Hospital, Department of Histology, Peterborough District Hospital, Thorpe Road, Peterborough PE3 6DA. Tel: 01733 874000. www.tissuebank. co.uk.

Probate Department, Principal Registry of The Family Division, 42–49 High Holborn, London WC4 6NP. Tel: 020 7947 6000.

The Terrence Higgins Trust, 52–54 Grays Inn Road, London WC1X 8JU. Tel: 020 7242 1010. www.tht.org.uk.

War Pensions Agency, Norcross, Blackpool FY5 3WP. Tel: 01253 858 858, 0800 169 2277. ukonline.gov.uk/dss.gov.uk.

# Index

accounts
 approval of, 104, 107
 form of, 104, 107
 preparation of, 104
 reconcilliation of, 107
advance directives, 15
advertisement for creditors
 and claimants, 70, 79,
 115–118
AIDS, 31
annulment of marriage
 effect on power of
  appointment, 89
 effect on appointment of
  spouse as guardian, 90
 effect on appointment of
  spouse as executor or
  trustee, 90
 effect on will, 89
assisting suicide, 14
authorised investments,
 100–101

bank account
 tracing missing accounts,
 58–59
 valuation, 60
bankrupt
 beneficiary, 80, 99
 creditor, 80
bankruptcy
 discharged debt, legacy to
  repay, 93
 search for, 80

basic care
 meaning of, 17
 withdrawal of, 17
beneficiaries
 bankrupt, 80, 99
 missing, 99
 under age, 94, 99
Benefits Agency, 10
bequest
 contrary to public policy,
  90
 inalienable, 90
 insufficient assets to pay,
  90
 irreconcilable, 91
 of items which no longer
  exist, 91
 of other people's property,
  92
 of several legacies to one
  legatee, 93
 to bankrupt, 80, 98
 to creditor, 80, 93
 to organisation which has
  ceased to exist, 91–92
 to persons of unsound
  mind, 99
 to persons who die before
  testator, 91
 to spouse of witness to will,
  90
 to underage beneficiary,
  99
 to witness to the will, 90